THE
HISTORY OF INDIA

AKBAR

BADAUNI

THE
HISTORY OF INDIA

As Told by Its own Historians
THE MUHAMMADAN PERIOD

THE POSTHUMOUS PAPERS
OF THE LATE

SIR H. M. ELLIOT

Edited by Prof. John Dowson

Second Edition

Published by

Gyan Publishing House
5, Ansari Road
Daryaganj, New Delhi-110002
Phone: 011-47034999, 9811692060
E-mail: books@gyanbooks.com

Distribution Network
gyanbooks.com
India, USA, Canada, UK, Australia, France

ISBN : 978-81-212-2776-6 (HB)
First Published, 1867

2nd Impression 2021

Printed at: Gyan Press, Delhi.

The
History of India
Author: Sir H. M. Elliot

THE HISTORY OF INDIA

As Told By Its Own Historians

THE MUHAMMADAN PERIOD

THE POSTHUMOUS PAPERS

OF THE LATE

SIR H. M. ELLIOT

Edited by Prof. John Dowson

Second Edition

PUBLISHERS' NOTE

This volume brings to a close the reign of Akbar which the previous three volumes, *Akbar* by Nizamud-d din Ahmad (2 volumes) and *Akbar-Nama*, by Abu-l Fazl left unfinished.

"Copious selections," says the Editor, "have been taken from the *Muntakhabu-t Tawarikh* by Abdu-l Kadir Badauni," who "introduces into his work much original matter; and all that he says about the personal affairs of the Emperor and his religious opinions is of great interest." . . . . "Some curious and interesting personal details have been derived from the Memoirs of Asad Beg, an officer in Akbar's service. His statements place the Imperial government in an unfavourable light, and are far from exalting the personal character of the monarch. The original writers upon the life and times of Akbar may now be considered as exhausted, for their writings have all been diligently searched, and there cannot remain much to be yet gleaned."

The following is a list of the articles in this volume with the names of the respective writers:

I. *Tarikh-i Badauni* by 'Abdu-l Kadir Badauni (Reprinted from Vol. V of original edition)—Sir H. M. Elliot and the Editor. II. *Waki'at-i Shaikh Faizi*—"Lieutenant" Prichard. III. *Wikaya'-i* Asad Beg—B. W. Chapman, a former Member of the B.C.S. IV. *Tarikh-i Hakki*—Reprinted from old volume. V. *Zubdatu-t Tawarikh*—Reprinted from old volume. VI. *Rauzatu-t Tahirin*—Reprinted from the old volume. VII. *Muntakhabu-t Tawarikh*—Reprinted from old volume. VIII. *Maasir-i Rahimi*—Reprinted from old volume. IX. *Anfa'u-l Akhbar*—Reprinted from old volume.

The articles No. II to IX have been reprinted from Vol. VI of the original edition. The *Ain-i Akbari* is the greatest monument of the reign of Akbar. Enriched with copious notes, it was first translated by Blochmann and published in the "Biblitheca Indica". That work supplies many of the deficiencies of the historians. Blochmann's *Ain-i Akbari* has already been published in two volumes.

CONTENTS

This history, by Mulla 'Abdu-l Kadir Muluk Shah of Badaun, is called by the author *Muntakhabu-t Tawarikh;* but many others have compiled works under that title, and the name most frequently given to it in Hindustan is *Tarikh-i Badauni.*

It is a general history of India from the time of the Ghaznivides to the fortieth year of Akbar; and, in the reign of the latter, it is especially useful, as correcting, by its prevalent tone of censure and disparagement, the fulsome eulogium of the *Akbar-nama.* Despite this systematic depreciation, it has been observed[1] that 'Abdu-l Kadir's narrative conveys a more favourable impression of the character of Akbar than the rhetorical flourishes of the Court journalist. It concludes with lives of the saints, philosophers, physicians, and poets of Akbar's reign.

'Abdu-l Kadir, poetically styled Kadiri, was born at Badaun in 947 or 949 H. His father, whom he lost in 969, was called Shaikh Muluk Shah, and was a pupil of the saint Bechu of Sambhal. 'Abdu-l Kadir, or Badauni as he is familiarly called, studied various sciences under the most renowned and pious men of his age, most of whom he enumerates in the third volume of the original edition of this work. He excelled in music, history, and astronomy; and on account of his beautiful voice he was appointed Court *Imam* for Wednesdays. Early in life he was introduced to Akbar by Jalal Khan Kurchi, and for forty years he lived in

[1] *Elphinstone, History of India, vol. ii., p.* 209. *Biographical Dictionary, L.U.K., vol. i. p.* 583. *Maasiru-l Kiram, p.* 52; *Tabakat-i Shah-Jahani, pp.* 224, 284; *Beale, p.* 291; *Mir-at-i Jahan-numa, Insha-i Nigar-nama, Tabakat-i Akbari, end of Dehli sovereigns.*

company with Shaikh Mubarak, and Faizi and Abu-l Fazl, the Shaikh's sons. But there was no real friendship between them, as Badauni looked upon them as heretics, and his notices of them are couched in bitter sarcastic terms.[2] Badauni died at the beginning of the seventeenth century. The *Tabakat-i Shah-Jahani* gives A.H. 1024 (1615 A. D.) as the year of his death.*

Badauni was a very learned man, and was frequently employed by the Emperor to make translations into Persian from the Arabic and Sanskrit, as in the case of the *Mu'jamu-l Buldan, Jami'u-r Rashidi,* and the *Ramayana*: yet, notwithstanding this employment, for which he acknowledges he received, in one present only, 150 gold *mohurs* and 10,000 rupees, besides a grant of rent-free land, his distinguished patron receives no favour at his hands. He wrote a work on the *Hadis* called *Bahru-l asmar,* and he composed a moral and religious work, entitled *Najatu-r Rashid,* which he wrote at the suggestion of his friend Nizamu-d din Ahmad, the historian, and which he must have completed very late in life, because the *Muntakhabu-t Tawarikh* is mentioned in it. He also informs us that he translated two out of the eighteen sections of the *Mahabharata,* and abridged a history of Kashmir, which, under the annals of A.H. 998, is said to have been translated from the original Hindi by Mulla Shah Muhammad Shahabadi,[3] but apparently not the *Raja-tarangini,* for the translation of that work is usually attributed to Maulana 'Imadu-d

[2]*The Editor's additions are almost wholly derived from Blochmann's notices in the Ain-i Akbari, vol. i. pp.* 104, 168.

**For date of Badauni's death* (1004), *See Journ. As. Soc. Beng. for* 1869, *p.* 143.

[3]*Rauzat-i Tahirin.*

din. According to Professor H. H. Wilson,[4] there were frequent remodellings or translations of the same work, but amongst those which he notices he does not mention one by Mulla Shah Muhammad Shahabadi.[5]

Many of the translations from the Sanskrit which were made about this period, and those of 'Abdu-l Kadir, probably, among the rest, appear to have been executed under the superintendence of Faizi, the brother of the minister Abu-l Fazl, and he is usually supposed to have been the first Musulman who applied himself to the language and literature of the Brahmins; but this seems to be a mistake.

The aversion with which 'Abdu-l Kadir Badauni regarded the Emperor and his able ministers arose, as he himself frankly confesses, from his own bigoted attachment to the most bigoted of religions, in which it was apprehended that Akbar, with their aid and countenance, was about to introduce some dangerous innovations.[6] He acknowledges, however, that he temporized and never hesitated to make his own religious views subordinate to the primary consideration of self-interest (and it is evident that envy of his fellow-courtiers, and discontent with the amount of favour bestowed upon his own unappreciated merits, were ever present in his mind, and embittered his feelings.)

Though the author of the *Tarikh-i Badauni* professes to derive his information chiefly from the *Tarikh-i Mubarak-Shahi* and the *Tabakat-i Akbari*,—indeed, in a passage in the *Najatu-r Rashid*,[7] he calls his work a mere abridgment of the *Tabakat*,—yet, contrary

[4]*Asiatic Researches, vol. XV. p.* 2.

[5]*See Ain-i Akbari (Blochmann's), vol. i. p.* 103.

[6]*See H. H. Wilson's works, vol. ii. p.* 379; *Blochmann's Ain-i Akbari, vol. i. pp.* 104; 167; *Journ. As. Soc. Bengal,* 1869.

[7]*MS. (Fol.* 26, *v.*).

to the usual Indian practice, there is much more original matter in it than such a declaration would lead us to suppose, and the whole narrative, even when avowedly taken from his predecessors, is tinged with his peculiar prejudices, of which many traits will be found in the extracts which are subjoined.

The history ends with the beginning of the year 1004 A.H. 1995-6 A. D. ("The book was kept secret, and according to a statement in the *Mir-atu-l 'alam,* it was made public during the reign of Jahangir, who showed his displeasure by disbelieving the statement of Badauni's children, that they had been unaware of the existence of the book. The *Tuzak-i Jahangiri* unfortunately says nothing about this circumstance; but Badauni's work was certainly not known in A. H. 1025, the tenth year of Jahangir's reign, in which year the *Ma-asir-i Rahimi* was written, whose author complains of the want of a history besides the *Tabakat* and the *Akbar-nama.*"[8]

The author gives the following account of his own work: "The writer, 'Abdu-l Kadir Muluk Shah Badauni, in obedience to the orders of His Majesty King Akbar, finished the abstract of the history of Kashmir in the year A.H. 999, which, at the request of the same monarch, was translated from Hindi into Persian by one of the learned men of his time; but as I cherished a great love for history from my very childhood, and as it was seldom that my hours were not employed either in the reading or writing some history, I often thought of compiling a brief account of the kings of Dehli, beginning from the commencement of the Muhammadan rule in India to the present time. . . . But circumstances gave me little opportunity of executing my desgin, and day after day I encountered numerous obstacles. Moreover, the scantiness of the means of subsistence obliged me to leave my country and friends, and thus the performance of

[8]*Blochmann, Ain-i Akbari, vol. i. p.* 104.

the work was for a time suspended, until my excellent and beloved friend[9] Nizamu-d din Ahmad Bakhshi went to Paradise. Excellent as is the history composed by this individual, yet I reflected that some additions could possibly be made to it; and I accordingly commenced to abstract briefly the accounts of some of the great kings of India, from the historical works called *Mubarak-Shahi* and *Nizamu-t Tawarikh Nizami*, sometimes adding my own observations. Great brevity has been observed in the style, and the use of figurative and flowery language throughout avoided. I have named this work *Muntakhabu-t Tawarikh*. It is hoped that this history, the object of which has been to place upon record the deeds of the great Muhammadan kings, and to furnish the means of transmitting my own reputation to posterity, will rather prove a source of my lasting happiness, than tend to aggravate my misfortunes.

"As it is my intention to write only what is true, I hope that God will forgive me, if I should ever allow myself to descend to the relation of minute and trivial particulars."

At the conclusion, he says that it was at one time his intention to have added a history of Kashmir, Gujrat, Bengal, and Sind, and an account of the wonders of India; but as they had no necessary connexion with the history of the Dehli Emperors, he changed his determination, and concluded his labours, in the year of the Hijra 1004, and as Nizamu-d din died in 1003, it would appear that he was only one year employed upon this

[9]*His warm friendship for Nizamu-d din has already been shown elsewhere, and it appears to have been reciprocated by Nizamu-d din; for in a passage in the Muntakhabu-t Tawarikh, we find that the Bakhshi had no scruple about giving in false returns, concealing the real cause of the absence of 'Abdu-l Kadir.*

history. But the preface is not very explict upon this point, and the meaning must be conjectured.

This is one of the few works which would well repay the labour of translation; but it would require a person to bring to the task a greater degree of knowledge of the Persian language than most Indian histories demand, as well as a thorough acquaintance with contemporary historians; for the author not only uses some uncommon words, but indulges in religious controversies, invectives, eulogiums, dreams, biographies, and details of personal and family history, which interrupt the unity of the narrative, and often render it a difficult matter to restore the broken links of connexion. Nevertheless, it must be confessed, that these digressions are the most interesting portion of his work; for rarely do the other obsequious annalists dare to utter their own sentiments, especially such as would be ungrateful to a royal ear, or to confess their own errors and foibles, as 'Abdu-l Kadir does with so much complacency and indifference. His own extensive knowledge of contemporary history also induces him very often to presume that his reader cannot be ignorant of that with which he himself is so intimately acquainted. He consequently slurs over many facts, or indicates them so obscurely, as frequently to compel a translator to supply the omissions from his own resources and conjectures.

The abstract of Indian History, from the Ghaznivide Emperors to Akbar—Akbar's history—and the Biographies of holy and wise men, physicians, and poets—each occupy about one-third of the volume, as will be seen from the subjoined abstract.[10] Almost all the headings have been added on the margin by a copyist, the author giving very few, except the names of kings and others whose lives he records; yet these must be of some

[10] *See Sprenger's Bibliog., p.* 55.

antiquity, as many copies concur in giving them in the same language and form.

CONTENTS: Reigns of the Ghaznivide Monarchs, pp. 4-21. Reigns of the Dehli Monarchs, pp. 21-133. From Zahiru-d din Muhammad Babar to Akbar, pp. 134-199. Jalalu-d din Muhammad Akbar. pp. 200-403.

DETAILS OF AKBAR'S REIGN

Mirza Sulaiman Kazi Nizam Badakhshi, alias Kazi Khan, deputed to negotiate peace—Death of Himun, the grocer, by the hand of the Emperor.—Khan-zaman's action with Hasan Khan Bachgoti.—Displeasure of Bairam Khan with Pir Muhammad.—Conquest of Gwalior.—An account of Shaikh Muhammad Ghaus of Gwalior.—Serious complaints to the Emperor against Khan-khanan.—An account of Ram Das, the second Tansen, and his receiving a present of a *lac* of rupees from Khan-khanan.—Birth-place of Amir Khusru.—Pir Muhammad Khan drowned.—Arrival of an ambassador from Shah Tahmasp Safwi.—Death of Muluk Shah, father of the author.—Maulana 'Alau-d din Lari.—Mirza Muhammad Hakim, son of Humayun Badshah.—Murder of the mother of Mirza Muhammad Hakim.—Marriage of the Emperor with the widow of 'Abdu-l Wasa'.—Death of Shah Abu-l Ma'ali.—Death of Shaikh Muhammad Ghaus.—Capital punishment of Kazi Lal.—Fort of Agra built.—The bard Mahapatar.—The Fort of Rohtas.—Mu'izzu-l Mulk and Raja Todar Mal put to flight by Khan-zaman and Bahadur Khan.—Khan-zaman and Bahadur Khan slain by the hands of the Emperor Akbar.—Capture of the fort of Chitor.—Mir 'Alau-d daula Kazwini, author of "Biographies of the Poets."—Death of Shaikh Abdu-l 'Aziz of Dehli.—Reduction of the fort of Rantambhor.—Fathpur.—Saiyid Musa falls in love with Mohani, a jeweller's daughter.—Death of Shaikh Gadai.—Birth of the Emperor Jahangir.—Capital punishment of Mirza Mukim

Isfahani.—Death of Shaikh Salim Chishti.—Conquest of Gujarat.—Birth of Prince Daniyal.—Death of Sultan Muzaffar Gujarati.—Erection of the fort of Surat, in defiance of the infidels of Faringistan.—Ibrahim Husain Mirza killed.—Capture of the fort of Nagarkot.—Birham Das, alias Birbal.—Forced march of the Emperor towards Gujrat.—Muhammad Husain Mirza killed.—Abu-l Fazl's first introduction to the Emperor Akbar.—Building of the fort of Payag, and the name of Illahabas given to it. —Capture of the forts of Hajipur and Patna.—*Singhasan Battisi*.—The Emperor goes on foot to visit the sacred sepulchre at Ajmir.—Jalal Khan killed.—Death of Khwaja Amina.—Fight of Khan-khanan with Daud Afghan, ruler of the territories of Orissa.—Abu-l Fazl's second introduction to the Emperor Akbar.—Opinions promulgated by Shaikh Abu-l Fazl.—Performance of the pilgrimage to Mecca discountenanced.—Translation of the *Hayatu-l Haiwan*.—Respecting the legality of temporary marriages.—Mulla Muhammad Yezdi arrives in India.—Translation of the *Atharva Veda*.—Fight with Rana Sanga.—Khan Jahan fights Daud Khan, who is seized and killed.—Death of Shah Tahmasp, King of Persia.—Death of Shah Isma'il the second, and accession of Sultan Muhammad, son of Shah Tahmasp.—Fight of Asaf Khan with the Raja of Idar.—The Emperor's indifference to the Muhammadan faith.—The ceremony of kissing the ground established as a mode of obeisance.—Abu-l Fazl translates the Gospel.—Birbal.—Worship of the Sun.—Abu-l Fazl appointed as superintendent of the temples of fire-worshippers.—Altercation between Abu-l Fazl and the compiler of this work.—Mian Tansen.—Arrival of an Ambassador from 'Abdu-lla Khan Uzbek. —The presentment made by the learned.—Muzaffar Khan killed in Bengal.—Death of Hakim Nuru-d din.—Arrival of Shaikh Muthi Afghan.—Khwaja Maulana Shirazi, the heretic, who knew the art of making amulets. —The author of this book, which is full of malignity, abuses Kazi 'Ali, of Baghdad.—Account of an organ.—Murder of Shah Mansur.—Controversy between Muhammadans and Christians.—A tavern built at the gate of the palace, and orders issued respecting the purchase of wine, and unlawful acts not prohibited.—Regarding certain jocular sayings.—Orders issued prohibiting the teaching of the commentaries and traditions.—Death of Makhdumu-l Mulk and Shaikh 'Abdu-n Nabi.—Death of Ghiyasu-d din 'Ali, Asaf Khan, and Shaikh Jalal Thanesari.—Arrival of Mir Fathu-lla Shirazi from the Dakhin.—Orders issued for the compilation of the *Tarikh-i Alfi*.—Translation of the *Mahabharat*.—Mian Tansen.—A brief account of Ram and his wife Sita.—Marriage of a daughter of Raja Bhagwan with Prince Salim.—Commencement of the second *karan*.—Death of Mirza Muhammad Hakim, son of the Emperor Humayun.—Birbal Killed.—Fight with the Roshanai Afghans.—Death of Abu-l Ghais Bukhari.—Assassination of the blessed Mulla Ahmad Thattavi by the merciless sword of an accursed pigling.—Translation of the *Ramayana*.—Death of Shah Fathu-lla Shirazi.—Death of Hakim Abu-l Fath.—Death of Todar Mal and Bhagwan Das.—Death of Shaikh Wajihu-d din.—Date of the death of Shahabu-d din Khan.—Death of Shaikh Ibrahim Chishti.—Death of Urfi Shirazi.—Death of Kazi 'Ali, of Baghdad, grandson of Kazi Husain.—Fight of Zain Khan with the Roshanai Afghans.—Death of Shaikh Mubarak Nagori.—Religious precepts.—Administrative orders.—Death of Nizamu-d din Ahmad.—Death of Shaikh Ya'kub Kashmiri.—Death of Hakim 'Ainu-l Mulk and Hakim Hasan Gilani.—The *Shahnama* turned into prose.—Death of Shaikh Faizi, son of Mubarak Nagori.—Death of Hakim Human.

Shaikhs and holy men, thirty-eight persons, pp. 403-434. Learned men, sixty-nine persons, pp. 434-477. Physicians, fifteen persons, pp. 477-480. Poets, one hundred and fifty-three persons, pp. 480-557. Conclusion, pp. 557-

562. Size—Folio, containing 562 pages, of 23 lines to a page.

The *Tarikh-i Badauni* is one of the commonest histories to be met with in India. One of the best copies is in the Asiatic Society's Library. Other good copies are to be found in Banda, Lucknow, Kole, and Patna. (The whole of the work has been published in three volumes in the Bibliotheca Indica, and many passages have been translated by Blochmann as notes to his edition of the *A'in-i-Akbari.*)

EXTRACTS

Muhammad Tughlik

(Text, vol. i. p. 227) In A.H. 729 Tarmah Shirin[11] the Mughal, brother of Katlagh Khwaja Mughal, King of Khurasan, who had on a previous occasion invaded Hindustan, advanced with a large army to the province of Dehli. He captured several forts, and committed ravages and massacres from Lahore, Samana, and Indri to the confines of Badaun, nor did he retreat till the victorious arms of Islam were arrayed against him. The Sultan pursued him as far as Kalanor, and leaving Mujiru-d din Aborja to dismantle that fortress, he returned towards Dehli.

At this juncture, it occurred to the Sultan to raise the taxes of the inhabitants of the Doab ten or twenty per cent., as they had shown themselves refractory. He instituted also a cattle-tax, and a house-tax, and several other imposts of an oppressive nature, which entirely ruined and desolated the country, and brought its wretched inhabitants to destruction.

IBRAHIM, SON OF SIKANDAR LODI

(Text, vol. i. p. 327.) Rai Bikramajit, who succeeded his father Rai Man Singh in the possession of Gwalior,

[11] "*Tarmsharin Khan.*"

found himself unable to withstand the royal troops, and was obliged to surrender the lofty edifice of Badalgarh,[12] one of the forts dependent on Gwalior, and built by Man Singh. On this occasion, a brazen figure which was worshipped by the Hindus fell into the hands of the Musulmans, which they sent to Agra. Sultan Ibrahim forwarded it to Dehli, and placed it before one of the gates of the city. Ten years before the compilation of this history, in the year 992, it was brought to Fathpur, where the compiler of this work saw it. Gongs, and bells, and all kinds of implements were subsequently manufactured from the metal of which it was composed. In those days Sultan Ibrahim, entertaining suspicions against his old nobles, fettered and imprisoned most of them, and transported others to various distant places.

SALIM SHAH, SON OF SHER SHAH SUR

(Text, vol. i. p. 384). Salim Shah,[13] in the beginning of his reign, issued orders that as the *arais* of Sher Shah were two miles distant from one another, one of similar form should be built between them for the convenience of the public; that a mosque and a reservoir should be attached to them, and that vessels of water and of victuals, cooked and uncooked, should be always kept in readiness for the entertainment of Hindu, as well as

[12]*("The cloud cap't tower.")—This was also the name of the old fort at Agra, which was evidently within the area of the present one, because Jahangir, at the opening of his memoirs, says, "My father demolished the old fort on the banks of the Jumna, and built a new one." It must, however, have been pretty nearly desroyed before Akbar's time, by the explosion.*

[13]*The correct name is Islam Shah, but some historians style him Salim, and most copies of the Tarikh-i Badauni pervert it still more by giving the name as Islim.*

Muhammadan, travellers. In one of his orders he directed that all the *madad-m'ash* and *aima* tenures in Hindustan which Sher Shah had granted, and all the *sarais* which he had built and the gardens he had laid out, should not be alienated, and that no change should be made in their limits. He took away from the nobles all the dancing girls maintained in their courts, according to the common practice of India. He also took from them all their elephants, and let none of them retain more than a sorry female, adapted only for carrying baggage.

It was enacted that red tents should be in the exclusive use of the sovereign. He resumed, and placed under the immediate management of the State, the lands enjoyed by the troops, and established pecuniary payments in lieu, according to the rates fixed by Sher Shah. Circular orders were issued through the proper channels to every district, touching on matters religious, political and fiscal, in all their most minute bearings, and containing rules and regulations, which concerned not only the army, but cultivators, merchants, and persons of other professions, and which were to serve as guides to the officials of the State, whether they were in accordance with the Muhammadan law or not;—a measure which obviated the necessity of referring any of these matters to *Kazis* or *Muftis*.

In order that these circular instructions might be fully comprehended, the nobles in command of five, ten or twenty thousand horse, were ordered to assemble every Friday in a large tent, within which was placed, on an elevated chair, a pair of Salim Shah's slippers, and a quiver full of arrows. They then bowed down before the chair, one by one, according to their respective ranks; first of all the officer in command of the troops and then the *munsif*, or *amin*, and so on; after which, with due respect and obeisance, they took their respective seats, when a secretary coming forward read to them the whole of the circular instructions above referred to, which filled about eighty sheets of paper. Every difficult point then at issue within the province was decided according to their purport. If any of the nobles committed an act in contravention of these orders, it was reported to the King, who forthwith passed orders directing proper punishment to be inflicted on the offender, as well as on his family. These rules were in force till the end of the reign of Salim Shah, and the compiler of this history witnessed the scene above described, when he was of tender age, that is, in the year 955 A.H., when he accompanied his maternal grandfather (may God extend his grace to him!) to the camp of Farid Taran, commander of 5,000 horse, which was then pitched in the district of Bajwara, a dependency of Bayana.

In the year 954 or 955 A.H. (God knows which year is correct) Khwaja Wais Sarwani, who was appointed to command the expedition against 'Azam Humayun, fought with the Niazis on the confines of Dhankot, and was defeated. 'Azam Humayun, flushed with this success, pursued the Khwaja as far as Sirhind. Salim Shah despatched a large force against the rebels, and a battle ensued at the same place, in which the Niazis were defeated. Some of their women who were made captives were sent prisoners to Gwalior, and Salim Shah violated their chastity. He distributed among the vagabonds of his camp the tents, standards, and other spoil of the Niazis which had fallen into his hands, bestowing upon them the titles which were common among the Niazis; such as Saiyid Khan, 'Azam Humayun, Shahbaz, etc. He granted them kettle-drums, which were beaten at their respective gates at the stated times. These low persons used to beat their drums aloud, and claim the dignity of the dogs of the celestial sphere. These people, in conformity with the practice of making rounds, which is occasionally observed among the prostitutes of India, went every Friday night to do homage to Salim Shah, instead of saying their prayers. On their arrival at the palace, the heralds exclaimed, "Oh king, be gracious enough to cast Your Majesty's eyes upon such and such Niazi Khans, who have come to offer up prayers for your health and welfare." This proceeding exceedingly disgusted the Afghans, who were of the same tribe as the King. The Niazi titles, and the standards and drums, which were granted to them by Salim Shah, are said by some historians to have been bestowed on them after the first battle. God knows whether this is correct or not. 'Azam Humayun, who was defeated in the last battle, was never able again to take the field.

The ranks of the Niazis began to be thinned day by day, and they soon dispersed. In the first instance they took refuge with the Ghakars, in the neighbourhhod of Rohtas, and then settled themselves in the hills in the vicinity of Kashmir. Salim Shah, with the view of suppressing for the future the disturbances excited by these insurgents, moved with an overwhelming force, and took up a strong position in the hills to the north of the Panjab, where, for the purpose of establishing posts, he built five fortresses, called Mankot, Rashidkot, etc. As he had no friendly disposition towards the Afghans, he forced them, for a period of two years, to bring stones and lime for the building of those fortresses, without paying them a single *fulus*, or *jital*. Those who were exempted from this labour were employed against the Ghakars, who resisted strenuously, and with whom they had skirmishes every day. At night the Ghakars prowled about like thieves, and carried away whomsoever they could lay hands on, without distinction of sex and rank, put them in the most rigorous confinement, and then sold them into slavery.

These circumstances sorely affilicted the Afghans, who felt that they were exposed to every kind of insult, but it was not in the power of any individual to lay their grievances before Salim Shah; until one day, when Shah

Muhammad Farmuli, a noble noted for his hilarity and jocular speeches, who was a special companion of the King, took heart and exclaimed, "O my liege! two nights I dreamt that three bags descended from heaven; one containing ashes; another, gold; and the third, papers; the ashes fell upon the heads of the troops; the gold upon the houses of Hindus; and the papers fell to the lot of the royal treasury." Salim Shah did not take the allusion ill, and it had the effect of inducing him to promise that he would, on his return to Gwalior, order his accountants to disburse two years' pay to the troops, but his death, which occurred soon afterwards, prevented the fulfilment of this promise.

SULTAN MUHAMMAD 'ADIL, OTHERWISE CALLED 'ADALI, SON OF NIZAM KHAN SUR

(Text, vol. i. p. 413.) His real name was Mubariz Khan; but when he ascended the throne, with the accord of the ministers and nobles, he assumed the title of Muhammad 'Adil. The people, however, used to call him 'Adali, and went so far as to alter the letters of this name and convert it into Andhali, which means "blind."

Ibrahim Khan, after an unsuccessful action at Khanwa, fled to Bayana, which is a strong fort in a commanding position. Himun immediately invested it, and skirmishes were of daily occurrence between the contending parties. The fort was well supplied with guns and ammunition, and Ghazi Khan, Ibrahim's father, who was in Hindun, used to throw supplies into it by way of the hills to the west of Bayana. Himun invested the fort for three months, and devastated the whole of the country in the neighbourhood, and my father's library in Basawar was almost entirely destroyed.

At this time a dreadful famine raged in the eastern provinces, especially in Agra, Bayana and Dehli, so that one *sir* of the grain called *juwari* rose to two and a half *tankas,* and even at that price could not be obtained.

Many of the faithful closed their doors, and died by tens and twenties, and even in greater numbers, and found neither coffin nor grave. Hindus perished in the same numbers. The common people fed upon the seeds of the thorny acacia, upon dry herbage of the forest and on the hides of the cattle which the wealthy slaughtered and sold. After a few days, swellings rose on their hands and feet, so that they died, and the date is represented by the words *khashm-i izad,* "Wrath of God." The author with his own eyes witnessed the fact that men ate their own kind, and the appearance of the famished sufferers was so hideous that one could scarcely look upon them. What with the scarcity of rain, the famine and the desolation, and what with uninterrupted warfare for two years, the whole country was a desert, and no husbandmen remained to till the ground. Insurgents also plundered the cities of the Musulmans.

Amongst the remarkable incidents of the year 962, during the war between Sikandar and Ibrahim, was the explosion in the fort of Agra, of which the following is a brief account. When the army of 'Adali Khan had left Agra, Ghazi Khan Sur sent his own officers with a garrison to protect the property, to keep the fort in a state of preparation, and to lay in provisions, for which purpose they had to examine the several storerooms and workshops. By chance, early one morning, as they were going their rounds with a lamp, a spark fell into a room filled with gunpowder. In the twinkling of an eye it ignited, and rising up to heaven, the earth quaked, so that the inhabitants of the city thought that the Day of Judgement had come, and prayed devoutly when they were roused thus suddenly from their slumbers. Planks, enormous stones and columns were sent flying several *kos* to the other side of the Jumna, many people were destroyed, and the limbs of men and of animals were blown away, full ten or twelve miles. As the name of the citadel of Agra was originally called Badalgarh, the date, 962, was found in the words *A'tash-i Badalgadh*—"The fire of Badal."

While Himun was encamped before Bayana, the people died with the word "bread" upon their lips, and while he valued the lives of a hundred thousand men at no more than barley-corn, he fed his five hundred elephants upon rice, sugar, and butter. The whole world was astounded and disgusted. Himun, once every day, would eat with his own followers in public, and calling the Afghans to his own table, he would invite them to eat, telling them to take up large handfuls, and he would shamefully abuse any one whom he saw eating slowly, and say, "How can you with such a slender appetite expect to fight with any rascally Mughal?" As the Afghans had now nearly lost their power, they could not muster spirit enough to reply to the unclean infidel; and laying aside the bluntness and hastiness for which they are so celebrated, they consented, whether from fear of consequences or hope of reward, to swallow his foul language like so many sweetmeats, adopting the following verses as their maxim:

"Place not your hands submissively on my feet;
Give me only bread, and lay your slipper on my head."

REIGN OF AKBAR

Campaign of Khan-zaman

(Text, vol. ii. p. 24. Year 964.) Khan-zaman in these few years, with a small force, fought bravely against the numerous forces of the Afghans, and obtained the victory over them. The history of his campaigns is a bright page in the annals of the time. At the battle of Lucknow Hasan Khan Bachgoti came up against him with 20,000 men, and Khan-zaman had not altogether more than 3000 or 4000. When the enemy passed the river Karwi and attacked Bahadur Khan, he himself was engaged taking a meal. When he was told that the enemy was at hand, he called for the chess-board and played at his ease.

Afterwards being told that a foreign army was driving back his forces, he called for his arms. His tents were being plundered, and his whole army was in confusion. He ordered Bahadur Khan to retire; then he, with a few men, beat his drums and fell upon the enemy. He overpowered them, and drove them for seven or eight *kos*. Many of them were slain, and heaps were formed of the corpses.

So also at Jaunpur he fought with the Gaurian who called himself Sultan Bahadur, and had issued coin and caused the *khutba* to be read in his name in Bengal. This man advanced against Jaunpur with about 30,000 horse, and the men of Khan-zaman were completely routed. When Khan-zaman arose from his repast, he found the enemy engaged upon their meal or occupied in plundering. The Khan fell upon them with a small party of men, completely routed the Afghans, killing many and making many prisoners. He obtained such booty that his army wanted for nothing. The victories which he and his brother achieved could have been accomplished but by few. These two brothers had many noble qualities; but the mark of rebellion was upon them, so that in the end all their exploits came to the dust.

GWALIOR AND RATAMBHOR

(Text, vol. ii. p. 31.) In the year 966 the fort of Gwalior was taken. A slave of 'Adali's named Buhail Khan (Suhail), being besieged in the fort, made terms and surrendered the keys. The date was found in the words, *Fath bab kil'ah Gwalior.* In this same year another slave of 'Adali's, named Sangram Khan, sold the fort of Rantambhor into the hands of Surjan Rai Hada. The facts of the matter are, that shortly before this, when His Majesty took up his abode at Agra, he sent a party of *amirs,* such as Hindu Beg Mughal, to reduce this fort. These *amirs* drove Sangram Khan before them, and ravaged the country round the fortress; but they were unable to accomplish their object.

AFFAIRS OF THE AUTHOR

(Text, vol. ii. p. 32.) In A.H. 966, I left my home at Basawar, and went to Agra, for the purpose of completing my education. I became acquainted with Mihr 'Ali Beg, and lived in his house. The Beg pressed most earnestly upon Shaikh Mubarak Nagori, my tutor (the peace of God be upon him!), and Muluk Shah, my father (God sanctify his tomb!), his desire that I should accompany him on his projected expedition, and threatened that he would not depart, unless this request was conceded. These two dear guardians, moved by their friendly feelings, being persuaded that it was to my advantage to go, consented to the arrangement, and to please them, though an inexperienced traveller, and though compelled for the time to relinquish my usual studies, I started, in the height of the rains, on this perilous journey. Passing through Kanauj, Lucknow, Jaunpur, and Benares, and seeing all that was to be seen, and holding interviews with several holy and learned personages, I crossed the river Ganges, and arrived at Chunar in the month of Zi-l ka'da, A.H. 966.

Jamal Khan sent some of his dependents to meet Mihr 'Ali Beg, and they conducted him to Jamal Khan's house. The palaces of Sher Shah and Salim Shah, and all the ammunition and resources of the fort were shown to him, and he was apparently received with the utmost hospitality and kindness.

When the *farman* was read, which was intended to conciliate Jamal Khan, by conferring upon him five *parganas* of Jaunpur in *in'am* tenure, in lieu of the fort of Chunar, Jamal Khan showed that he had further expectations, and placed the most unheard-of difficulties in the way, seeking to delay Mihr 'Ali until an answer should be received to the representation which he had made to Court. He insidiously wrote also, at the same time, communications both to Khan-zaman and to Fath Khan Afghan, who was in the fort of Rohtas with a considerable force, holding out to them separately promises of the fort.

When Mihr 'Ali was aware of the perfidy practised by Jamal Khan, and being not without suspicions of the fidelity of Fath Khan, he feared they would league together for his injury, and so he left the fort under pretence of taking an airing, and crossing the river in considerable alarm, proceeded direct to Agra,[14] leaving me in the fort. As I thought it best to temporize with Jamal Khan by way of making my own escape, I proposed to him that I should try and bring back Mihr 'Ali, and effect a reconciliation. To this he acceded, and in the evening I got into a boat with the intention of crossing the river. It so happened that the boat fell into a raging whirlpool under the hill near the wall of the fort, and a fierce wind arose which made the vessel shiver. If the mercy of God, the ruler of earth and water, had not acted as my sail, the bark of my hope would have been dashed to atoms by the whirlpool of calamity against the hill of death.

In the jungle which lies at the foot of the Chunar hills, Shaikh Muhammad Ghaus, one of the greatest saints of India, had resided for twelve years in the practice of asceticism, consuming the leaves and fruits of the forest as his food; and so celebrated was he for the fulfilment of his blessings, that even powerful kings used to come and visit him, and pay their respects. I fell in with one of his dependents, and arrived at the hermitage. He himself was not there, for in this very year he had proceeded from Gujarat to Agra, where he arrived in great pomp and circumstance, accompanied by several disciples,

[14] *This sentence is not in the printed text.*

and gave considerable satisfaction to the Emperor by the principles and faith which he professed. . . .

Shaikh Gadai, with that spirit of jealousy, spite, and malice which is a peculiar failing of the saints of Hindustan, was vexed at this intrusion of a rival, and looked upon Shaikh Muhammad Ghaus as one shopkeeper does on another, who commences the same trade, in the storey directly over his head. Wise men know well the truth of the adage, "Two of a trade never agree." Khan-i khanan, who was much attached to Shaikh Gadai, did not receive Shaikh Muhammad with that degree of respect and favour which was his due. On the contrary, he assembled divines and learned men, in order to ridicule the treatise of the Shaikh, in which he had said that he had in his waking moments had an interview and conversation with God, who assigned him a superiority over the Prophet Muhammad. He had written other nonsense equally pernicious and blasphemous. He sent also for the Shaikh, and made him the butt of his contumely—so that the Shaikh, much chagrined, retired to Gwalior, where he engaged himself in the pursuits of his holy calling, and contented himself with the proceeds of a *jagir*, which yielded a *kror* (of *tankas*).

(Text, vol. ii. p. 53.) On 27th Rajab of this year (969 A.H.) my father Muluk Shah (may God be merciful to him !) died in Agra of dysentery. I carried his bier to Basawar, and there buried him. I found the date of his death in the words *Jahan-fazl*.

(Text, vol. ii. p. 63.) At the time when the compiler of this work resided at Agra, for the purpose of finishing his education Shaikh Muhammad Ghaus one day passed by in great state, and accompanied by acclamations which rent the air. He was clothed in the garb of a *fakir*. I was at first anxious to pay my respects to him; but when I learnt that he was in the habit of rising to receive the salutations of Hindus, that desire vanished, and I was deprived of the satisfaction I had anticipated. Another day, I saw him in the *bazar* at Agra, with multitudes of people thronging before and behind him, and he was so constantly occupied in returning the salutations of the people on all sides of him, that he could not sit up erect during the whole time of his airing. Although he was eighty years old, his countenance was wonderfully fresh, and his whole appearance betokened anything but old age and debility. The mèrcy of God be upon him![15]

(Text, vol. ii. p. 64.) On the 20th of the blessed month Ramazan of this year (970 A.H.) I heard at Sansawan, in Sambal. of the death of my maternal grandfather in Basawar. He had taught me several sciences, and I was much attached to him. He had many claims upon the respect of men of letters. The date of his death is represented by the letters composing the words, *Fazil-i Jahan*, "The excellent of his time."

HUSAIN KHAN TUKRIYA

(Text, vol. ii. p. 125.) In A.H. 977 the *pargana* of Lucknow was transferred from the possession of Husain Khan Kashmiri to that of Mahdi Kasim Khan, who had just returned from Mecca, and had paid his respects to the Emperor at Rantambhor. Husain Khan[16] was high-

[15]*Among the biographies which are given at the close of the work, one is devoted to the Shaikh, in which the author says, that there was so little pride and self-sufficiency in the Shaikh's composition, that he was never known to utter the monosyllable "man", I. The instance he adduces to prove the assertion is, by the studied attempt to avoid the use of that word, more offensive than the most rampant egotism.*

[16]*This man, of whom some notice has already been taken in the Tabakat-i Akbari, appears to have been an enthusiast, or a mad man, who could not get over the persuasion that inexhaustible wealth was to be procured, from possessing himself of the mines in the hills. Five or*

ly indignant at this, and exclaimed, "Our friendship is broken, we shall meet no more till the day of judgement." He then abandoned in disgust (his wife) the daughter of Mahdi Kasim, notwithstanding he loved her, and took the daughter of his uncle Ghazanfar Beg. After a while, leaving his wife in distress, and the daughter of Mahdi Khan with her brothers in Khairabad, he set forth from Lucknow with the design of breaking down the idols and of demolishing the idol temples. For he had heard that their bricks were made of gold and silver, and other false reports of their unbounded treasures had come to his ears. He proceeded through Oudh, towards the Siwalik hills.[17] Hhe hillmen, as is their custom, abandoned the lower hills after a slight resistance, and fled for security to higher elevations, of which the ascent was very dangerous. Husain

six years afterwards, he plundered the Doab, and then made an attack on Basantpur in the hills, where there was a royal garrison, and died from the effects of a gun-shot wound received there. 'Abdu-l Kadir, who declared himself a devoted friend and admirer of Husain Khan, says that, though to all appearance he was a fool, he was in reality a very intelligent man. See Infra.

[17]*An impression of the great wealth of Kumaun was generally prevalent about this time. Firishta at the conclusion of his work, in speaking of the native Rajas of Hindustan, says, "The Raja of Kumaun possesses extensive dominions. A considerable quantity of gold is procured by washing, and copper mines are to be found in the country. The treasures, too, are vast. It is a rule among the Rajas not to encroach upon the hoards of their ancestors; for it is a saying among them, that whoever applies his father's treasures to his own use, will become mean and beggarly in spirit, so that, at the present day, fifty-six distinct treasures exist, which have been left by the Rajas of Kumaun, each with the owner's seal upon it."*

Khan arrived at last at the place where Sultan Mahmud, nephew of Pir Muhammad Khan, was slain. He read the *fatiha* for the pure spirits of the martyrs who fell there, and repaired their dilapidated tombs. He then ravaged the whole country as far as the *kasbah* of Wajrail, in the country of Raja Ranka, a powerful *zamindar,* and from that town to Ajmir, which is his capital. In that place are to be found mines of gold and silver, silks, musk, and all the productions of Tibet, from which country he was only distant two days' journey—when, on a sudden, as has been frequently observed in those mountains, the neighing of the horses, and the sound of the kettle-drums, as well as the voices of his followers, caused the clouds to collect, and so much rain fell, that neither corn nor grass was to be procured.[18] Famine stared the army in the face, and although Husain Khan, with the most undaunted intrepidity encouraged his men, and excited their cupidity by representing the wealth of the city and the country, in gold, jewels and

[18]*This story reminds us of the succour which was so opportunely offered to the army of Marcus Aurelius, when it was engaged in a hopeless conflict with the Marcomanni, in the barren mountains beyond the Danube.*

Oh nimium dilect Deo! cui fundit ab antris
Æolus armatas hiemes: cui militat æther,
Et conjurati veniunt ad classica venti.

Claudian, De tert, Cons. Honor. v. 98.

Tertullian, Eusebius, Jerome, and other Christian authors ascribe the miraculous shower to the prayers of the Christian soldiers in the army. Suidas and Dio Cassius to a magician. The fact is indisputable; the cause is more probably explained by our Oriental writer. In modern days, it has frequently been observed that severe actions have been followed by rain, and philosophical reasons have been assigned for this curious effect.

treasure, they were too much disheartened to second his resolution, and he was compelled to retreat.

On their retreat the Kafirs, who were in possession of the passes, showered down stones and arrows tipped with poisoned bones upon them. They also blocked up the way, and most of the bravest of his warriors drank the cup of martyrdom. Many of the wounded, who escaped at the time, died five or six months afterwards from the effects of the poison.

Husain Khan returned to Court, and requested that Kant and Gola[19] might be conferred upon him in *jagir,* in lieu of the one he held before. This was graciously acceded to. Several times he made incursions to the foot of the hills with various success, but he was never able to penetrate into the interior. Many fine fellows, who had secaped half-dead from his first expedition, now felt the malarious influence of the climate, and died off, but not in battle. After some years Husain Khan, contrary to the advice and remonstrances of his friends, mustered his forces for a final struggle to get possession of the hills, and perished in the attempt. as, please God, will be mentioned in its proper place.

About this time I went, after taking leave of Husain Khan, from Lucknow to Badaun, where I formed a suitable nuptial alliance for my brother, Shaikh Muhammad, whom I loved from my very soul, nay, better than my own soul, for he was endowed with every excellent and angelic quality. Three months did not elapse before he died, he as well as 'Abu-l Latif, the light of my eyes, the earliest fruits of the garden of my life (my first-born), who, when time cast an evil eye upon him, was carried

[19]*This district, which pretty nearly corresponds with Shahjahanpur, in Rohilkhand, is sometimes styled Kant Gola.*

off, in the twinkling of an eye,[20] from the cradle to the tomb, and I was suddenly reduced from the happiest to the saddest of men. God created me, and to God shall I return!

Death of Shaikh Salim Chishti.—The Author wounded.—Conflagration at Badaun

(Text, vol. ii. p. 136.) In the year 979 A.H. the palace at Agra and the palace at the new town of Fathpur were completed . . . . At the close of the month of Ramazan of this year, Shaikh Salim Chishti, of Fathpur, died. He was one of the chief saints of Hindustan, and his sayings are worthy of commemoration. I will hereafter give notice of him, please God, in the supplement to this history.

During this year an unfortunate accident befell the author, of which the following are the particulars. At the period when Kant and Gola was held in *jagir* by Muhammad Husain Khan, and when it pleased fate to associate me with him for some time, as I was appointed Judge of that district,[21] I went on a pilgrimage to Makanpur, a dependency of Kanauj, where is the tomb of the holy Shaikh, Badi'u-l Hakk wau-d din Shah Madar (may God sanctify his tomb!). This son of man, through the disposition which he inherited from his sinful and ignorant nature (which he imbibed with his mother's crude milk, and which is the cause of shame and reproach), and through innate darkness and ignorance (which are the source of presumption and baseness, and which came down to him by inheritance from father Adam), the eyes of his wisdom were covered with a film

[20] *This triple repetition of the word "eye" is intended for a witticism—frigid enough, and in a most inappropriate place.*

[21] *wa faqir ism sadarat-i-un subah wa uhdah khidmat faqra dasht.*

of lust, and he was inclosed in the net of lasciviousness, so that he committed all of a sudden, as was of old fore-willed by Providence, a gross impropriety within that shrine. Since the chastisement as well as the mercy of God was upon me, I received upon earth the punishment of my sin, by his ordaining that several connexions of the girl whom I fell in love with should inflict nine sword wounds upon my head, hands, and shoulders. They were all slight, but one penetrated the bone of my skull, and reached to the brain, exposing me as a brainless fellow, and another partially severed the veins of the little finger of my left hand. I fainted away, and appeared to be travelling to another world. My God bless my resurrection!

I met with an excellent surgeon in Bangarmau, who closed my wounds within a week, and in the midst of my pain and illness, I made a vow, that if I recovered I would go to Mecca—a vow which I have not yet been able to perform, but which I hope, God willing, to do before I die, and before any obstacle intervenes to prevent the execution of that excellent resolve. The rest is with God!

Afterwards, I arrived at Kant and Gola, and had no sooner bathed after my recovery, than I was again laid on my bed by sickness, the wound having become ulcerous from the effect of excessive cold. Husain Khan (may God bless him with eternal Paradise! for he showed himself more than a father or a brother to me) administered some medicine, in the shape of a plaster and electuary, both made from the wood of the tamarisk, and enabled me to proceed on my journey to Badaun. There another surgeon took off the dressings, and re-opened the wound on my head. I was nearly expiring from the intensity of the pain . . . . .

During this year a dreadful fire broke out at Badaun, and an immense number of Musulmans and Hindus perished in the flames. Carts full of the remains of those who were burnt were driven down to the river, and no one could tell who was a believer, and who an infidel. Many who escaped being burnt rushed to the ramparts, and were so scorched by the flames, that men and women precipitated themselves from the wall in despair. Some had their skins burnt and disfigured. Water seemed only to add fuel to the flames. All this I witnessed with my own eyes, and heard the noise of the flames with my own ears. Some it warned, others it destroyed. A short time before this, a half-witted fellow came from the Doab, whom I took into my own house and society. He said to me one day in private, that I ought to flee out of that city, as some infliction of Providence was about to befall it. But I paid no attention to him, as he was a frequenter of taverns.

ERECTION OF THE FORT OF SURAT, IN DEFIANCE OF THE PORTUGUESE INFIDELS

(Text, vol. ii. p. 145.) One day in the year 980, the King went to look at the fort of Surat, and gave orders to repair the portions that had been battered and destroyed. During his inspection he saw the large mortars, which had been despatched with a powerful fleet and army by Sulaiman Sultan, the Turkish Emperor, to assist in capturing the harbours of Gujarat, and had been left on the sea-shore, covered with rust, because Sulaiman Aga, the admiral, had abandoned the enterprise through meeting with some obstacle.[22] There they remained, until Khuda-

[22]*Muhammadan authors slur over the precipitate retreat, but Shaikh Zainu-d din confesses to a panic.—See Rowlandson, Tohfut-ul-mujahideen, p.* 143. *Maffei —who styles the admiral Sulaiman, "Solimanus Peloponnesius, vir enormi non minus adipe, quam avaritia et crudelitate notissimus,"—tells us, that the Turks were so terrified by the four lanterns, which the Portuguese*

wand Khan *wazir* had them carried into the fort of Surat, at the time it was building. The few which remained had been taken to Junagarh[23] by the Governor. The King

hung out from some of the ships of the Goa fleet, that they set sail for Arabia in the utmost alarm, leaving behind them five hundred wounded and a great portion of their ordnance.

Nonnius, (Nuno de Cunha) dum ab subsidium inclusis ferendum reliquam ornat classem, celeriter præmissæ liburnicæ sexdecim ad Madrafabam accesserant noctu, quaternis in singulas puppes luminibus ad speciem augendam haud frustra sublatis: eo quippe terrore Turcæ perculsi, tribus jam millibus suarum amissis, . . . noctis intempestæ silentio conscendunt naves, duobus circiter mensibus in obsidione consumptis; ac vela dant in Arabiam tanta cum trepidatione, ut saucios quingentos et magnam tormentorum partem fæde reliquerint.—(Maffei, Hist. Indič. Lib. xi. vol. ii. p. 503.)

Diego de Conto says that the stratagem was rendered more effectual by the coincidence of an eclipse of the moon.—("Asia," Dec. v. lib. v. cap. 4. *See also Faria-e-Souza, tom. i. part iv. cap.* 9.)

"Solyman, the Bassa," says Knolles, "a most famous Pyrat, assaulted (in September, 1538) *Dium, a castle of the Portugals, situate upon the mouth of that great river (Indus), but, in conclusion, after he had many days besieged the castle, both by sea and land, and tried the uttermost of his strength, he was so repulsed by the Portugals, that he was glad to forsake the siege, and leaving his great ordance behind him for haste, returned back again to Aden, a city of great trade in Arabia Felix."—Turkish History, vol. i. p.* 451.

[23]*Firishta, in his reign of Mahmud Shah III. of Gujarat, says that they were brought "from" Junagarh for the defence of Surat; and this is the most probable, as the ordnance was abandoned at Diu.*

inspected them, and gave orders that some of them, which were not wanted there, should be sent to Agra.[24]

The reason assigned for Khudawand Khan's[25] building the fort of Surat is, that the Firingis used to oppress the Musulmans in every kind of manner, devastating the country, and tormenting God's servants. At the time of laying the foundations of the fort, they tried to throw every obstacle in the way, by firing cannon from their ships,[26] but all without effect.

The expert engineer laid the foundations of one side within the sea, dug a deep ditch round the two sides which faced the land, and built the walls with stones and burnt bricks. The wall was thirty-five yards long.[27] The breadth of the four walls was fifteen yards, and their height twenty yards, and the breadth of the ditch was twenty yards. All the stones, the joints and interstices were fastened together with iron clamps, and made firm with molten lead. The battlements and embrasures are lofty, and so beautiful that every one was astonished at beholding them. On the bastions, which projected into the sea, was erected a gallery (*ghurfa*), which the Firingis, especially the Portuguese, profess to say is an invention of

[24]*The "Mir-at-i Ahmadi" says there was only one Sulaimani gun which the King wished to transfer to Agra, but could not find the means of transport for so heavy a piece.—See Bird, History of Gujarat, p.* 322.

[25]*This is the same chief that we read of in Sidi 'Ali's journal.—See Diez, Denkwurdigkeiten von Asien, vol. ii. p.* 180.

[26]*atash bazi bisiyar bikushtiha sar dadand.*

[27]*This sentence was not given in the original translation, but a note in the printed text says that it is found in all the three copies consulted. There must be some omission or error, or the fort must have been a very small affair.*

their own. When the Musulmans began to erect this *chaukandi,*[28] the Firingis exerted every kind of opposition to obstruct it; and when they found they could not prevail by force, they offered large sums of money to prevent its being built: but Khudawand Khan, through the regard

[28]*It is quite incomprehensible why this building, whatever it was, should have excited so much rancour on both sides. One might suppose it was rather a battery, than a small palace. Literally, it may be said to mean "a four-cornered room." Briggs calls it a four-storied palace. He translates the passage thus: "Within the town is a beautiful building, four stories high, which the Hindus call Chowkunda, and the Europeans campare it to a Portuguese palace. Finding they could not prevent by force the construction of the fort, the Portuguese offered large sums of money to induce Khoodabunda Khan not to fortify Surat, but their gold was rejected."* —(*Briggs, vol. ii., Firishta, vol. iv. p.* 147.)

This differs much from the original, which runs thus: "The Firingis said, 'If you will not abstain from building the fort, do not, at any rate, build the chaukandi after the model of Portugal; and to secure that, we will pay as much money as we offered to prevent your building the fort.' Ghazanfar Akai Turk, surnamed Khudawand Khan, replied, 'Through the liberality of the Sultan I am in need of nothing; and to show my detestation of you, I shall build this kind of chaukandi, and secure for myself the peculiar blessings which attend good works.' He then sent for the ordnance and other stores, which were called Sulaimani on account of the Turks having abandoned them, and which were then in Junagarh, and placed them in different parts of the fort of Surat, and strengthened it."—(*History of Gujarat, Mahmud Shah III.*)

I cannot find mention of the transaction in any European author.

which he bore to his own religion, sternly refused, and plied the work till it was finished, in contemptuous defiance of the Christians.

HUSAIN KHAN TUKRIYA

(Text, vol. ii. p. 151.) In 980 A. H. Husain Khan Mahdi Kasim Khani, *jagirdar* of Kant and Gola, had gone off to quell the insurgents of Badaun and Pattiali, before he heard of Ibrahim Husain Mirza's arrival in the neighbourhood of Dehli. In the mean time, Makhdumu-l Mulk Maulana 'Abdu-lla Sultanpuri and Raja Bihar Mal, who were entrusted with the chief direction of affairs during the King's absence in Gujarat, wrote to Husain Khan from Fathpur, to inform him that Ibrahim Husain Mirza had experienced two defeats, and was then in the vicinity of Dehli, and that as no person of importance was now present to defend the capital, he ought to hasten to Fathpur without delay.

He accordingly prepared to obey their summons, and was well on his road, having arrived at the village of Oudh, in Jalesar, when he learnt that the Raja of Awesar still continued the depredations which he had practised since the accession of the King, in the neighbourhood of Agra, and had become a predatory robber (*kazzak*). He had been engaged in several hard conflicts with some loyal nobles, and had slain many excellent men, and at that time he was concealed in the jungle of the village of Naurahi, in the *pargana* of Janesar.

We had scarcely time to ponder on this intelligence, when all of a sudden, while we were marching at mid-day on the 15th of Ramazan, the men being off their guard, and going on in separate parties, most of them, also, being exhausted with the fast, an attack was made upon us, with matchlocks and arrows. The Raja of Awesar had formed stages of wicker-work on the tops of the trees, and from this secure position several of our men were killed and wounded. At the very commencement of the attack, a ball struck Husain Khan below the knee, grazed his thigh, and, passing through the saddle, was spent upon the head of his horse. He was very nearly fainting and falling from his saddle, but his self-possession enabled him to keep his seat by clinging to the pommel. I threw water on his face, and his immediate attendants, not aware of the accident, at first thought that his fasting had worn him out. I then seized hold of his bridle, for the purpose of carrying him for safety behind a tree out of the storm of arrows, when he opened his eyes, and, contrary to his usual habit, looked sternly at me, and made signs that there was no need to hold his reins, but that we should dismount and join in the fray. We accordingly alighted, leaving him there to take care of himself.

The contest then raged with fury, and many were killed on both sides. At last, towards evening, victory inclined to our party, which was the smallest, and the infidels were put to flight like so many sheep, but not before our *sipahis* were so tired, that they could scarcely wield a sword or shoot an arrow. We had all been so jammed together in the forest, that we could with difficulty tell friend from foe. Some of our men had strength of mind and body enough, to deserve the reward, both of engaging in holy war, and of maintaining a strict fast. I, on the contrary, in my weakness, at last took a cup of water to moisten my throat, for the want of which some poor fellows died.' Several excellent friends of mine attained martyrdom in repelling this attack.

After this victory, Husain Khan returned by rapid marches to Kant and Gola, and strengthened those places. Shortly after, Ibrahim arrived in the *pargana* of Lakhnor, fifteen *kos* from Sambal.[29] As Husain Khan was still suffering from the effects of his wound, he was obliged to

[29] *Sambal was the paternal estate of Ibrahim Husain Mirza. Gulrukh Begam, his wife, was a daughter of Kamran Mirza, and, consequently, Akbar's first cousin.*

be carried on a litter, but nevertheless he advanced to Bans Bareilli, in order to force Ibrahim to action, and from Bareilli he made Sambal in one day by a forced march. Ibrahim, alarmed at this exhibition of confidence and courage, thought it better to decline an action, and retreated by way of Amroha, in the environs of Lakhnor, leaving a distance of seven *kos* between him and his opponent. Had Husain Khan been compelled to fight in his then wounded state, God knows what would have happened! It was one of the Mirza's mistakes that he did not attack Husain Khan while he was in this weak state.

Mu'inu-d din Khan Farankhudi, governor of Sambal, with a large party, and several other *amirs* and *jagirdars* of the neighbourhood, who had taken refuge in the fort, when they heard at midnight the roll of the drums of Husain Khan, they thought the Mirza was upon them, and were quite overpowered by fear. But when the cry arose that Husain Khan had come to their assistance, they came out joyfully to meet him. Next day we went to the abode of Shaikh Fathu-lla Tarbati, one of the vicars of Shaikhu-l Islam Fathpuri, and there held a council. It was then considered advisable that all the *amirs* of the neighbourhood of Dehli who had turned out against the Mirza should go with Tolak Khan Korchi and . . . to the *pargana* of Ahar on the Ganges, and there wait for us; then, after the junction of the forces, further operations might be decided on.

Husain Khan exclaimed, "Good God! The Mirza came here with a small party of horse, and although your numbers more than doubled his, you took refuge in the fort of Sambal; and now twenty or thirty *amirs* and old soldiers with a large force are so dismayed that you want to shelter yourselves in the fort of Ahar, which is a mere rat's hole. This will encourage the Mirza to make further attacks upon the Imperial territories. Now there are two courses open, one of which we must fellow. You must cross the Ganges, and, under the cover of that old fort, must intercept the Mirza, and prevent his getting over the Ganges. I will follow up in his rear, and we shall see what will happen. Or I will hasten over the Ganges and head the Mirza, while you pursue him. This seems to be our duty." But they could not agree upon any course until Husain Khan, driven by necessity, went off in haste with the horsemen he had to the *amirs* at Ahar, and inveighed loudly against their going into the fort. He brought them out, and again held a council with them. "The enemy," he said, "is in the heart of the country, and is like a hare in the midst of a camp. If we follow him up sharply, we may settle his business, and take him alive. The glory of this victory will be yours." The soldiers said, "Under the orders of Makhdumu-l Mulk and Raja Bihar Mal, we have driven the Mirza out of the Dehli territory, and have come into Sambal. Mu'inu-d din Ahmad Khan is the master and *jagirdar* of this province, and he is now responsible. Our orders were to protect Dehli, not to make war upon the Mirza, for there are risks in such a course."

Intelligence now arrived that the Mirza had attacked Amroha, and having crossed the Ganges at the ford of Chaubala, was marching rapidly towards Lahore. Husain Khan, convinced of the apathy of the *amirs,* separated himself from them immediately, and made a forced march to Garh-muktesar, in order to arrest the Mirza. Of the royal *amirs,* Turk Subhan Kuli and Farrukh Diwana were the only ones that accompanied him. A letter now reached him from the *amirs* of Ahar, urging him to come, speedily and join them. The Mirza, like the rook on a cleared chess-board, now came into the heart of the country, plundering and ravaging the towns in his way. When he was at Payal, his men committed such atrocities upon Musulman people as cannot well be described. In that town twelve virgins were ravished with such violence that several of them died. Other places fared in the same way. Husain Khan followed the steps of the Mirza, and the *amirs* came after him, until they reached Sirhind. Here they became refractory, and would go no further. But Husain Khan was not content to remain. With the small force under his command, not exceeding 200 men in all, and with the two persons (above named), he marched rapidly from Sirhind to Ludiyana. There he learnt that on the Mirza's approaching Lahore, the garrison had closed the gates against him. Upon this the Mirza went to Sher-garh and Jahni.

Husain Kuli Khan, who was besieging Nagarkot and the fort of Kangra, heard of these movements of the Mirza's; so he patched up a treaty with the Hindus. He received five *mans* of gold as tribute from the people of Nagarkot, and had the *khutba* read in His Majesty's name. He then marched away along with Mirza Yusuf Khan, Masnad-i 'Ali, Fattu (Katlu) the slave of 'Adali, Ism'ali Khan, Raja Birbal and other *amirs,* and proceeded in pursuit to Sankra. When Husain Khan heard of this movement, in that madness which a thousand times had got the better of his judgement, he swore an oath that he would not eat food until Husain Kuli joined him. Crossing the Biyah at the ford of Talwandi, he made a forced march to Sher-garh, one of the dependencies of Jahni. There he paid a visit to Shaikh Daud Kadiri Jahni-wal. When food was served, he excused himself from eating on account of his oath. The Shaikh observed that it was easy to atone for an oath, but silly to distress one's friends. The Khan instantly called for a slave, and having set him free, thus atoned for his oath. Then he partook of the food, and benefited by the gracious words which he heard. He remained there that night. The monastery of the Shaikh provided entertainment for all the party, and his fields furnished grass and corn for the horses.

Three days afterwards I came from Lahore to Sher-garh, and stayed there four days, seeing and hearing things which had never entered into my imagination. I was anxious to withdraw from the world, and to devote myself to the sweeping of the monastery. But the Shaikh would not allow me, and told me I must go to Hindustan. So I took my leave in a very forlorn and distressed state. . . .

One stage from Talwandi, Husain Khan addressed a letter to Husain Kuli Khan, saying that he had come four hundred *kos* by forced marches, and begging for one day's delay, so that he might join him, and share in the victory to be won. Husain Kuli Khan said, "Very well," and sent the messenger back. On the same day he hastened on to the town of Tulamba, four *kos* from Multan, and attacked the Mirza, who was out hunting, and quite unaware of his approach. Some of the Mirza's men were preparing to march, and others had dispersed, and were not in condition to fight. Mas'ud Husain Mirza, younger brother of Mirza Ibrahim Husain, took the initiative, and attacked the forces of Husain Kuli Khan; but his horse stumbled and fell upon the broken ground, and he was taken prisoner. When Mirza Ibrahim Husain returned from hunting, all chance was gone; and although he fought well, and made several charges, he was unable to gain any success; so he turned his reins and fled.

The day after the victory Husain Khan arrived at Tulamba, with eighty or ninety men, and drums beating. Husain Kuli Khan showed him the battle-field, and told him of each man's exploits. Husain Khan then said, "As the enemy has escaped alive, you must pursue him and take him prisoner, for the business is not yet completed." Husain Kuli Khan replied that he had come from Nagarkot by forced marches, that his forces had suffered many hardships in that mountainous country, and were not in condition. A complete victory had been secured, and now there was an opportunity for other friends.

Husain Khan now hoped that his turn was come, and

that the hardships and the forced march of five hundred *kos* had opened a way for him, so he took his leave, and pressed forward. Some men, who were worn out with fatigue, he sent to Lahore with the elephants and drums. With a small party of men he took up the pursuit of the Mirza. There was but a short distance between him and the unfortunate Mirza, when one night the Mirza and about four hundred horsemen halted on the banks of the Biyah and Sutlej, where the rivers unite. The *jhils,* who are a low class of Multan peasants, having collected together, made a night attack upon him, and assailed him with arrows. The Mirza, with a party of men, some wounded and some disabled, did what they could to beat off their assailants; but the *jhils* came on successfully. At length an arrow, guided by fate, struck the Mirza at the back of his head, and came out through his throat. Unable otherwise to help himself, he changed his clothes, and his men left him. They fled, sorely distressed, in every direction. But wherever they went, they were marks for the arrows of death, and met their fate. One or two old slaves of Mirza Ibrahim, having dressed him in the garments of a *kalandar,* were desirous of getting him out of the way of danger. His helplessness was so great that they took him for refuge to the dwelling of a *darwesh* named Shaikh Zakariya. Outwardly the Shaikh applied ointment to his wounds, but privately he sent information to Sa'id Khan at Multan. The Khan sent a slave named Daulat Khan to bring in the Mirza a prisoner. Sa'id Khan wrote a despatch, and sent it to the Emperor as he was coming to Ajmir on his return from Gujarat.

Husain Khan, when he heard of the capture of the Mirza, hastened to Multan, and saw Sa'id Khan. He made a difficulty about seeing the Mirza, and said: "If when I see him, I salute him, it will be inconsistent with my duty to the Emperor, and if I do not salute him, it will be uncourteous, and the Mirza will say to himself— 'See this uncircumcised fellow, who, when he received quarter at the siege of Satwas, made obeisances without end, and now that evil days are fallen upon me treats me cavalierly.' " The Mirza heard these ceremonious words of his, and said "Come and see me, and without obeisance, for I waive it." Notwithstanding he made his bow, and saw him. The Mirza, with an anxious look, said, "I had no intention of rebellion and disturbance. When the matter took a serious turn, I took my own course, and threw myself into a foreign country. But they would not allow me to stay there. If it was my fate that this defeat should fall upon me, would to God that I had received it at your hands that it might have been the cause of the advancement of you, who are my co-religionist, and not from Husain Kuli Khan, who is alien in religion and sect!" Husain Khan then returned to Kant and Gola, and soon afterwards he heard that the Mirza had died in prison.

Husain Khan proceeded from Kant and Gola to Court. Husain Kuli Khan also came to Fathpur from the Panjab, bringing Mas'ud Husain Mirza, with his eyes fastened up, and a number of the Mirza's men as prisoners. They were nearly three hundred persons, and they were brought before the Emperor, with skins of asses, hogs, and dogs cast over them, some to be put to death with divers tortures, and some to be set at liberty . . . . Sa'id Khan also sent the head of Mirza Ibrahim Husain from Multan, having had it cut off for the purpose after his death.

SULAIMAN KIRANI

(Text, vol. ii. p. 163.) In this year (980) died Sulaiman Kirani, ruler of Bengal, who had assumed the title of *Hazrat-i 'ala.* He had conquered that mine of infidelity, the city of Katak and Banaras,[30] and had made Jagannath a home of Islam. His authority extended from Kamru

[30]*Katak was called "Katak Banaras."*

(Kamrup) to Orissa. His son Bayazid succeeded him; but in the course of five or six months, the Afghans put him to death, and his brother Daud bin Sulaiman attained the sovereignty.

ABU-L FAZL

(Text, vol. ii. p. 173.) About this time (Zi-l hijja, 981 A.H.), Shaikh Abu-l Fazl, son of Shaikh Mubarak Nagori, the star of whose knowledge and wisdom was brilliant, came to Court, and received many marks of distinction.

BUILDING OF PALACES

(Text, vol. ii. p. 173.) In 981 fine spacious palaces were built on the road to Ajmir. His Majesty's devotion induced him every year to go on a pilgrimage to that city. So directions were given for building a palace at every stage between Agra and Ajmir, and for erecting a pillar and sinking a well at every *kos*. Some hundreds of thousands of stags' horns, which had been killed in the course of His Majesty's life, were placed upon the pillars as a memorial for the world.[31] Would that, instead of these, gardens or *sarais* had been formed!

LODI AFGHAN

(Text, vol. ii. p. 174.) Daud was now at Hajipur, and at the instance of Katlu Khan, governor of Jagannath, he threw into prison his *amiru-l umara* Lodi, who had been ruler of Orissa, but who had since taken a hostile course, and had set himself up in opposition in the fort of Rohtas. He got Lodi into his power by holding out the bribe of an elephant. They tell the story that one day Daud went out hunting with a small escort, and that

[31] *The pillar, which is in the best state of preservation, is to be seen at Fathpur Sikri, where the garrulous cicerone gives a very different account of its origin. It is called "hiran minar," or "pillar of the antelope."*

Lodi, with ten thousand horsemen of Sulaiman's, formed the design of putting down Daud. But Daud went back to the city, assembled his forces, and scattered Lodi's followers. By his crafty management, he got Lodi into his power, and appropriated all that he possessed. Lodi, knowing his death to be certain, did not withhold his advice from Daud. He said, "Although I know that you will be very sorry after my death, and that you will derive no benefit from it, still I will give you one counsel, which if you act upon you will prove victorious. My advice is, that you place no reliance upon that peace which I effected not long ago by means of two *lacs* of rupees. The Mughals will never let you alone for this trifling sum. Be beforehand with them, and make war with them immediately, for there is nothing like the first blow." Daud thought he had an evil design in what he said, and, proud of the hollow peace which he had made with Khan-khanan, but which was no better than a shadow, he put the devoted Lodi to death. Thus he struck his own foot with the axe, and at the same time uprooted the plant of his prosperity with the spade of calamity.

BUILDING OF THE FORT OF PAYAG

(Text, vol. ii. p. 176.) On Safar 23rd, A.H. 982, His Majesty arrived at Payag (Prayaga), which is commonly called Illahabas, where the waters of the Ganges and Jumna unite. The infidels consider this a holy place, and with the object of obtaining the rewards which are promised in their creed, of which transmigration is one of the most prominent features, they submit themselves to all kinds of tortures. Some place their brainless heads under saws, others split their deceitful tongues in two, others enter hell by casting themselves down into the deep river from the top of a high tree.[32] Here His

[32]*Here is still further testimony to this tree being in*

Majesty laid the foundations of an Imperial city, which he called Illahabas.

TRANSLATION OF THE "SINGHASAN BATTISI"

(Text, vol. ii. p. 183.) In Jumada-l akhir, while the Court was at Sher-garh, otherwise called Kanauj, a book called *Singhasan Battisi,* which is a series of thirty-two tales about Raja Bikramajit, King of Malwa, and resembles the *Tuti-nama,* was placed in my hands; and I received His Majesty's instructions to make a translation in prose and verse. I was to begin the work at once, and present a sheet of my work on that very day. A learned brahman was appointed to interpret the book for me. On the first day I completed a sheet, containing the beginning of the first story, and when I presented it, His Majesty expressed his approbation. When the translation was finished, I called it *Khirad-afza,* a name which contains the date of its composition. It was graciously accepted, and placed in the Library.

REVENUE ARRANGEMENTS

(Text, vol. ii. p. 189.) In this year (982) an order was promulgated for improving the cultivation of the country, and for bettering the condition of the *raiyats.* All the *parganas* of the country, whether dry or irrigated, whether in towns or hills, in deserts and jungles, by rivers, reservoirs, or wells, were all to be measured, and every such piece of land as, upon cultivation, would produce one *kror* of *tankas,* was to be divided off, and placed under the charge of an officer to be called *krori,* who was to be selected for his trustworthiness, and whether known or unknown to the revenue clerks and treasurers. So that in the course of three years all the uncultivated land

the open air, at the point of the confluence, to a very late period. It is the celebrated Akhai-bar, or immortal fig-tree. See Wilson's Hindu Theatre, vol. i. p. 302.

might be brought into cultivation, and the public treasury might be replenished. Security was taken from each one of these officers. The measurement was begun in the vicinity of Fathpur. One *kror* was named Adampur, another Shethpur, another Ayubpur, and so on, according to the names of the various prophets (and patriarchs). Regulations were circulated, but eventually these regulations were not observed as they ought to have been. A great portion of the country was laid waste through the rapacity of the *kroris,* the wives and children of the *raiyats* were sold and scattered abroad, and everything was thrown into confusion. But the *kroris* were brought to account by Raja Todar Mal, and many good men died from the severe beatings which were administered, and from the tortures of the rack and pincers. So many died from protracted confinement in the prisons of the revenue authorities, that there was no need of the executioner or swordsman, and no one cared to find them graves or grave-clothes. Their condition was like that of the devout Hindus in the country of Kamrup, who, having dedicated themselves to their idol, live for one year in the height of enjoyment, appropriating everything that comes to their hands; but at the end of the period, one by one they go and assemble at the idol temple, and cast themselves under the wheels of its car, or offer up their heads to the idol.

[33]All the country, with the exception of that which was under the *khalisa* (exchequer), was held in *jagir* by the *amirs.* But from the prevalence of indulgence and debauchery, extravagance in household expenditure, and accumulation of riches, there was no means of maintaining the soldiery or of fostering the peasants. When the services of the *amirs* were required, they came into

[33]*Since translating these passages, I find that Blochmann has also translated this and several of the following paragraphs. See Ain-i Akbari, vol. i. p. 242.*

the field attended only by a few slaves, or some young Mughal soldiers. Able soldiers were nowhere to be found. Shahbaz Khan, the *mir-bakhshi,* revived the regulations of the *dagh* (branding), and the *mahalli,* which were instituted by Sultan 'Alau-d din Khilji, and were afterwards maintained by Sher Shah. It was also settled that every *amir* should be first appointed commander of a score (*bisti*)[34]. . . . When he brought up the horses of those twenty horsemen for the *dagh* according to the regulation, he might be promoted to be a *sadi* (commander of a hundred) or higher.

They were also to keep elephants, horses, and camels suitable to their rank. When they brought this number of horsemen for inspection, they were to be treated according to their deserts and position, and might attain to a *mansab* of 1000, 2000 or of 5000, than which there is none higher. If they did not do so, they fell from their rank.

But under this regulation also the ill-used soldiers fared worse. For it was found that the *amirs,* having effected their objects, dressed up many of their dependents (*khass-khailan*) and horsemen (*bargir*) in the garb of soldiers, and bringing them to the muster, they made up the complement of their *mansab,* and received *jagirs* in proportion. Then they dismissed the *bargirs* until they required them again, when they would once more enlist, according to their requirements, a number of temporary soldiers, and dismiss them again when no longer wanted.

The treasure, the collections, and the expenditure of the *mansabdars* remained unaltered, but in every way dirt fell into the plate of the poor soldier, so that he was unable to gird up his loins. Tradesmen, such as weavers, cotton-dressers, carpenters, and Hindu and Musulman grocers (*bakkal*) would hire a horse or

[34]*Here follows an unintelligible passage.*

charger, and bringing it up for the *dagh,* would obtain a *mansab,* and would become a *krori, ahadi* (guardsman), or *dakhili* (substitute) of some one. A few days afterwards no trace would be found of the hired horse or of the missing charges, and they were reduced to the position of footmen.

There were many men who at the time of the royal inspection at the public office were placed in the scales, bound hand and foot with their garments on, and their weight would reach to two and a half *mans* or three *mans* more or less. Afterwards it would be found out that the clothes were hired, and the horse borrowed. His Majesty used to say, "I with my eyes open, and aware of what I am about, give something to these men, so that they may have some means of living." After a while they would present themselves again as *ahadis* of two horses, of one horse, or even of half a horse. For two horsemen would be partners of one horse, and receiving for it the forage allowance, amounting to six rupees, would divide it between them. This sort of trade was carried on to a great extent; but for all this the Emperor's good fortune was so great and flourishing that his enemies were everywhere annihilated, and soldiers were not so much wanted. The *amirs* also were set free from the unseemly blandishments of the uncircumcised.

ABU-L FAZL'S SECOND INTRODUCTION TO AKBAR

(Text, vol. ii. p. 198.) In 982 Abu-l Fazl, now styled *'Allami* or "very learned," came a second time to Court. He set the world in flames, and "lighted up the lamp of the *Sabahis,"*—a proverbial way of saying he lighted his lamp by daylight. In accord with the saying, "He who contends gains his object," he set himself in opposition to all sects, and bound the girdle of reform about his loins. He presented a commentary on the *A'yatu-l kursi,* which treated on the nice points and subtleties of the Kuran. People say that his father wrote it, but he presented it, and got much praise. The words "*tafsir-i Akbari*" give the date of its composition. The Emperor received him graciously, and (in order to humiliate the arrogance of the proud *mullas*) looked upon him more favourably than he did upon me. The reason of Abu-l Fazl's antagonism and rancour was that at the time of the persecution and massacre of heretics like Mir Habshi and others, Shaikh Abdu-n Nabi, Makhdumu-l Mulk, and the learned in general took counsel together, and with one accord they represented that Shaikh Mubrak Mahdawi also was a heretic, who was lost himself, and led others to perdition. Having got tacit permission to repress and remove him, they sent officers to apprehend him; but as the Shaikh had absconded with his sons, they broke the pulpit of his mosque. He then sought the protection of Shaikh Salim Chishti in Fathpur, who was then at the height of his prosperity and eminence. Shaikh Salim sent him something for his expenses, and recommended him to leave the country, and fly to Gujarat. As he obtained nothing in this quarter, he went to Mirza 'Aziz Koka, who represented to the King, that Shaikh Mubarak was a learned and indigent man, that his children were clever, that he held no land in *in'am,* and inquired what was the advantage of persecuting a worthy man. So the Emperor gave up the intention of hurting him, and in a short time everything went on to his heart's content. Shaikh Abu-l Fazl ingratiated himself with His Majesty by his unremitting devotion to the King's service, by his temporizing disposition, by his duplicity, by his study of the King's temper and sentiments, and by his boundless flattery. When he at last obtained the opportunity, he took his revenge upon that sect whose works and efforts have met with so little reward. He was the cause not only of the destruction of these old labourers, but of the disasters which fell upon all God's wise and holy servants, upon the infirm and upon orphans, by the resumption of their allowances in money and rent-free lands. . . . When trouble and misery fell upon them, he used frequently to quote this quatrain:

"*I have set fire to my barn with my own hands,*
As I am the incendiary, how can I complain of my enemy?
No one is my enemy but myself,
Woe is me! I have torn my garment with my own hands."

If any one, while remonstrating, cited the precepts of religious men, he would say in reply, that the precept quoted was the composition of such and such a grocer, such and such a cobbler, such and such a currier, for he thought proper to reject all the wise sayings of Muhammadan Shaikhs and Doctors.

THE 'IBADAT-KHANA—POLEMICAL DISCUSSIONS

(Text, vol. ii. p. 200.) In the year 983 the buildings of the *'ibadat-khana* were completed. The cause of their erection was this. In the course of the last few years the Emperor had gained in succession many great and remarkable victories, and his dominion had grown in extent from day to day. Not an enemy was left in the world. He had taken a liking for the society of ascetics and the disciples of the celebrated Mu'iniyyah (God rest his soul!). He spent much time in discussing the Word of God and the sayings of the Prophet; and he devoted his attention to questions of *Sufism,* science, philosophy, law and other matters. He passed whole nights in meditation upon God and upon the modes of addressing him as *ya hu* and *ya hadi*. Reverence for the great Giver filled his heart. In order to show his gratitude for some of his blessings, he would sit many a morning alone in prayer and mortification upon the stone bench of an old cell which lay near the palace in a lonely spot. Thus engaged in meditation, he gathered the bliss of the early hours of dawn. . . . .

Having completed the building (of the *'ibadat-khana*), he made a large hall in each of the four divisions of it. He also finished the construction of the tank called *anuptalao*. He called the building *'ibadat-khana*, and by degrees it became at last a.........[35] . On Fridays after prayers he would go from the new *khankah* of the Shaikhu-l Islam, and hold a meeting in this building. Shaikhs, learned and pious men, and a few of his own companions and attendants, were the only people who were invited. Discussions were carried on upon all kinds of instructive and useful topics. . . . . . Every Sabbath evening he invited *saiyids, shaikhs,* doctors and nobles. But ill feeling arose in the company about the seats and order of precedence, so His Majesty ordered that the nobles should sit on the east side, the *saiyids* on the west, the *'ulama* on the south, and the *shaikhs* on the north. His Majesty would go from time to time to these various parties, and converse with them and ascertain their thoughts. Quantities of perfume were used, and large sums of money were distributed as rewards of merit and ability among the worthy people who obtained an entry through the favour of the Emperor's attendants. Many fine books which had belonged to 'Itimad Khan Gujarati, and had been acquired in the conquest of Gujarat, were placed in the royal library, but were subsequently brought out and distributed by the Emperor among learned and pious men. Among the rest he gave me a book called *Anwaru-l mashkut*. . . . . One night the vein of the neck of the *'ulama* of the age swelled up, and a great outcry and tumult arose. This annoyed His Majesty, and he said to me (Badauni), "In future report

[35]*The meaning is here doubtful. The text has three variant readings, 'ibadat, 'iyadat, and 'ibarat-khana, no one of which seems applicable.*

any one of the assembly whom you fiud speaking improperly, and I will have him turned out." I said quietly to Asaf Khan, "According to this, a good many would be expelled." His Majesty asked what I had said. When I told him, he was much amused, and repeated my saying to those who were near him.

He used to summon Makhdumu-l Mulk Maulana 'Abdu-lla Sultanpuri to that assembly, in order to annoy him; and he set up to argue against him Haji Ibrahim and Shaikh Abu-l Fazl, then a new arrival, but now the prime leader of the New Religion and Faith, or rather the infallible guide and expositor *de omnibus rebus et quibusdam aliis.* His Majesty used to interrupt the Maulana at every statement, and at a hint from him his companions also would interfere with interjections and observations, and would tell queer stories about the Maulana, and exemplified in his person the verse of the Kuran, "And some of you shall have life prolonged to a miserable age."

THE PILGRIMAGE

(Text, vol. ii. p. 203.) One night (during the year 983), Khan Jahan mentioned that Makhdumu-l Mulk had given an opinion that in those days it was not a religious duty to go on a pilgrimate, and that it was even sinful to do so. When he was asked his reasons, he replied, that there were only two ways to Mecca, one by 'Irak, the other by Gujarat. By the former, a man must hear abusive language from the Kazilbashes (Persian Shi'as); by the latter, he must, before he embarks at sea, suffer the indignity of entering into an engagement with the Firingis, which engagement was headed and stamped with portraits of the Virgin Mary and Jesus Christ (upon whom be peace!), and so is tinctured with idol worship.[36] Therefore both ways should be prohibited.

[36]*Maffei mentions a toll, and Osorius tells us that*

Another device of Makhdumu-l Mulk's was the trick by which he avoided payment of the legal aims due upon his wealth.[37] At the end of each year he used to make over all his property to his wife, but before the year had run out he took it all back again. It was said that he practised some other tricks, of which even the Israelites would have been ashamed. Stories were told, one after another, about his meanness and shabbiness, and baseness and worldliness, and oppression, all which vices were exhibited towards holy and deserving men, especially those of the Punjab, and which one by one came to light, verifying the saying, "There is a day when secrets shall be disclosed." They told also other stories founded upon his villany, sordid disposition, and contemptible conduct, and they ended by deciding that he ought to be shipped off by force to Mecca. When he was asked if he thought the pilgrimage a duty for himself, he replied in the negative. About this time, Makhdumu-l Mulk began to fall into discredit, and Shaikh 'Abdu-n Nabi[38] succeeded him in the good graces of the King.

the Portuguese allowed no one to sail without one of their passports. Faria-e-Souza says that these passports were not unfrequently mere "letters of Bellerophon," to the effect that "The owner of this ship is a very wicked Moor; I desire that the first Portuguese captain to whom this is shown may make a prize of her!"—See Rowlandson, Tohfut-ul Mujahideen, pp. 90, 104.

[37]*Or, more familiarly, how he avoided payment of income-tax.*

[38]*An account of each of these ecclesiastical judges is given among the Biographies of learned men at the end of the original work. That of 'Abdu-n Nabi will be found among these Extracts.*

Respecting Mukhdumu-l Mulk, an intelligent author, who has written on the subject of Akbar's deflec-

RENT-FREE TENURES

(Text, vol. ii. p. 404.) This year the King gave orders that the rent-free land throughout his dominions, whether in the shape of *ayma, madad-m'ash, uakf* or pensions, should not be considered valid, and that the revenue-officers should not recognize them until the *Sadr* had approved the grants. The consequence was, that the people whose rights were assailed flocked from the farthest east of India, and from Bakkar in the west, to represent their grievances. Whoever found a powerful friend among the nobles and people at Court, secured his wishes, and whoever could not obtain a similar introduction, had to give large bribes to Saiyid 'Abdu-r Rasul, and all the subordinates of the Shaikh, even to

tions from the path of the Muhammadan religion, observes: "A learned and pious writer, Makhdumu-l Mulk, published about this time a tract injurious to Shaikh 'Abdu-n Nabi. He accused that teacher of having been wrongfully instrumental to the deaths of Khizr Khan Shirwani, who had been condemned for reviling the Prophet, and 'Ali Habsh, who had been charged with heresy. He added also, that the Shaikh was unworthy to mount the pulpit, both because he was subject to a bodily infirmity, and because he had been disavowed by his own father for his perverse and undutiful conduct when a youth. To these attacks Shaikh 'Abdu-n Nabi replied by calling Makhdumu-l Mulk a heretic and a fool. Opinions were divided, some of the religious men sided with one, and some with another; the dispute ran high, and a complete schism ensued. The enemies of Islam took this opportunity to augment the King's disgust and dissatissatisfaction, and those impressions becoming progressively more intense, he lost in the course of five or six years every particle of his original belief."—Oriental Quarterly Magazine, vol. i. p. 51.

the *farashes,* door-keepers, grooms and sweepers, and by these means contrived at last to "save his blanket from the whirlpool." He who could not succeed in procuring either of these passports, was well thrashed and kicked by the attendants; besides which, many of the unfortunates perished from the effect of the hot air in that immense crowd. Although the King knew all these particulars, yet such was his regard for the *Sadr,* that he could not be persuaded to interfere with his proceedings. Whenever the *Sadr* sat in state and dignity in the *diwan-khana,* and held public audience, the nobles would, now and then, taking forward some learned and respectable man, represent his case for consideration. But he used to receive them with little respect, and after much entreaty and importunity, some able man, who could explain the *Hidaya,* or any equally abstruse book, would get a paltry hundred *bighas,* more or less, restored to him, and the rest, of which he might have been in possession for many years, would be resumed. But the ordinary run of ignorant and worthless fellows, even down to Hindus, would get as much land as they asked for, without question. From these proceedings, learning and its professors declined in estimation every day. Even in the middle of assemblage, while seated "aloft in awful state," if the time for midday prayers came, he would wash his hands, and care not how much water he sprinkled on the faces and clothes of the surrounding nobles and courtiers. They meekly submitted to the indignity, because they knew it was to the advantage of their poor clients, and would bestow upon the *Sadr* every kind of eulogium, compliment, and flattery, to his heart's content, in the hope by this means to secure at last some compensation for the insult.[39] In the time of no former

[39]*This last sentence is a free rendering of a rather offensive expression.*

king had any *Sadr* such extensive powers and jurisdiction.

THE AUTHOR'S APPOINTMENTS AND EMOLUMENTS

(Text, vol. ii. p. 206.) About this time the King appointed me a preacher, and directed me also to undertake the office of marking the royal horses with the brand. I had no fixed salary, but I was told from the first to act like a *mansabdar* of twenty in bringing horses to the brand. Shaikh Abu-l Fazl arrived at Court about the same time, so that we were, as was said, loaves out of the same oven. Yet he, beginning his service by marking horses and attending to the *mahalli,* managed by his intelligence and time-serving qualities to raise himself to a *mansab* of two thousand, and to the dignity of *wazir.* But poor I, from my inexperience and simplicity, could not manage to advance myself. I reflected within myself that there were still hopes of securing contentment (that best of possessions!) by means of a *madad-m'ash,* which would enable me to retire from the world, and apply myself to study and devotion, while free from the cares of the world. But even in this I was doomed to be disappointed.

In the month of Shawwal, 983, on my applying for leave of absence, it was refused; but I received a horse with suitable trappings, and a grant of a thousand *bighas,* which was a mere nothing, being only equal to an allowance for the maintenance of twenty men, but in accordance with the unfriendly disposition of the *Sadr* and my unlucky fate. It was styled also in the grant a *madad-m'ash.*[40] I represented that with this small tenure I could not afford to be constantly in attendance at Court, to which the King replied, that he would give me presents also during the marches.

[40] *That is, an eleemosynary grant, not a mansab or military tenure indicative of dignity.*

Shaikh 'Abdu-n Nabi too observed, that no person of my quality had received from him so large a grant of land. As for the presents which I was promised, though twenty-two years have elapsed since my hopes were raised, I have received them but once or twice, and the rest have been conceled behind the veil of fate. These fine promises were nothing better than a baseless mirage. I have performed services without reward, and undergone restraints, from which I can now be relieved only by the goodness of God.

"Allahu Akbar"

(Text, vol. ii. p. 210.) In these days (A.H. 983, A.D. 1575-6) His Majesty asked how it would be if he oidered the words *Allahu Akbar*[41] to be engraven on his Imperial seal and stamped upon his coins. Several people said it would be very good. But Haji Ibrahim objected. He said the phrase had an ambiguous meaning, and that it would be better to substitute the verse of the Kuran, *Lazikru Allahi Akbaru* ("To think of God is the greatest thing"), because it was free from ambiguity. His Majesty was not pleased with this, and said it was self-evident that no creature, in the depths of his impotence, could advance any claim to Divinity. He had only looked upon the word as being apposite, and there could be no sense in straining it to such an extent.[42]

THE EMPERMR'S HERETICAL ASSOCIATES

(Text, vol. ii. p. 211.) In this year (983) there arrived Hakim Abu-l Fath Gilani, Hakim Humayun (who subsequently changed his name to Hamayun Kuli, and lastly to Hakim Humam), and Nuru-d din, who as a poet

[41] *The signification usually attached to these words is "God is great"; but the meaning "Akbar is God" may be given to them.*

[42] *See Blochmann's Ain-i Akbari, vol. i. p. 166.*

is known under the name of Karari. These three were brothers, and came from Gilan (near the Caspian). The eldest brother, by his subserviency, obtained an extraordinary ascendancy over the Emperor. He flattered him openly, adapted himself to every change in the religious ideas of His Majesty, and pushing forward, he soon became a most intimate friend of Akbar. Soon after there came to Court Mulla Muhammad of Yazd, who got the nickname of *Yazidi*. He attached himself to the Emperor, and concocted the most extravagant censures against the *sahaba* (companions of the Prophet, the peace of God be upon them!). He told extraordinary stories (about them), and tried hard to make the Emperor a *shi'a*. But this man was soon left behind by Birbal, that bastard, and by Shaikh Abu-l Fazl and Hakim Abu-l Fath. They turned the Emperor from the Religion, and made him a perfect sceptic of inspiration, the prophetic office, the miracles and wonders, and the law. They carried matters to such a length that I, the author, could no longer bear them company. The result of all this, as regards each one of them, will be told in its proper place. About the same time, His Majesty ordered Kazi Jalau-d din and several other learned men to write a commentary upon the Kuran, but they fell to squabbling about it. That scoffer, Deb Chand, Raja of Manjhola, used to say, that if the cow had not been greatly esteemed by the Almighty, she would not have been mentioned in the first chapter of the Kuran. As history was read from day to day, His Majesty's faith in the Companions of the Prophet began to be shaken, and the breach grew broader. The daily prayers, the fasts, and prophecies were all pronounced delusions as being opposed to sense. Reason, not revelation, was declared to be the basis of religion. Europeans also paid visits to him, and he adopted some of their rationalistic tenets.

DEATH OF DAUD AFGHAN

(Text, vol. ii. p. 238.) In the early part of the engagement, a cannon-ball struck the knee of Junaid, and broke his leg. When the armies closed, defeat fell upon the Afghans. The horse of Daud stuck fast in the mud, and Hasan Beg made Daud prisoner, and carried him to Khan-jahan. The prisoner, being oppressed with thirst, asked for water. They filled his slipper with water, and took it to him. But as he would not drink it, Khan-jahan supplied him with a cupful from his own canteen, and enabled him to slake his thirst. The Khan was desirous of saving his life, for he was a very handsome man; but the nobles urged that if his life were spared, suspicions might arise as to their loyalty. So he ordered him to be beheaded. His execution was a very clumsy work, for after receiving two chops he was not dead, but suffered great torture. At length his head was cut off. It was then crammed with grass and anointed with perfumes, and placed in charge of Saiyid 'Abdu-lla Khan.

PERSONAL TO THE AUTHOR

(Text, vol. ii. p. 252.) In A.H. 985 the King, after visiting the shrines of the holy saints in the neighbourhood of Dehli, went towards Palam on a shooting excursion. At the close of the blessed month Ramazan, news reached me at Rewari, that at Basawar[43] a son had been born to me, of which happiness I had been a long time in expectation. On this occasion I presented an offering of a gold *ashrafi* to the King, and requested he would be good enough to name the child. After reading a prayer, he inquired the name of my father and grandfather. I replied, Muluk Shah was my father, and he was

[43]*This place, which is so frequently mentioned in the course of this history, is within the territory of Bharatpur, on the road from Agra to Jaipur. It is situated on the side of a rocky eminence, with a ruinous palace on its summit. Heber calls it Peshawar. See Narrative of a Journey, vol. ii. p. 385.*

the son of Hamid." He said, "I call your son 'Abdu-l Hadi," Hadi being a name which at that time he had, night and day, upon his lips. Notwithstanding that Hafiz Muhammad Amin, the preacher, was constantly citing the seven *imams,* urging me in high-flown language not to commit this absurdity, and to invite some learned men to my house to read the whole Kuran, in order to secure a long life to my son, he could not persuade me, and at the end of six months my son died. May God be pleased on his account to pardon me in the day of judgement!

From Rewari I took five months' leave, and went to Basawar, on account of sundry affairs of consequence, but I unavoidably extended my absence to the period of a year. This unwarranted neglect of duty and the machinations of my enemies made me fall in the King's estimation, and by degrees I was entirely forgotten. To this day even, although eighteen years have since elapsed, I still perform my duty, but am not honoured with an interview; and I can neither go in search of other employ, nor maintain a firm footing in my present position.

RENT-FREE TENURES

(Text, vol. ii. p. 254.) Kazi 'Ali Baghdadi, grandson of Mir Kazi Husain Maibazi, was deputed to the Punjab to make inquiries respecting the lands held in rent-free tenure, under the name of *madad-m'ash* and *ayma.* He was directed to resume the old tenures, to measure them, and to include them all in one district. The greatest anomalies had been perpetrated in this department, which were all to be attributed to the perversity of Shaikh 'Abdu-n Nabi and the dishonesty of his subordinates.

RELIGIOUS DIFFICULTIES

(Text, vol. ii. p. 255, A.H. 986.) His Majesty used frequently to go to the *'ibadat-khana*, and converse with the *'ulama* and the *shaikhs*, especially on Sabbath evenings, and would sometimes pass the whole night there. The discussions always turned upon religion, upon its principles, and upon its divarications. The learned doctors used to exercise the sword of their tongues upon each other, and showed great pugnacity and animoisty, till the various sects at length took to calling each other infidels and perverts. . . . Innovators and schismatics artfully started their doubts and sophistries, making right appear to be wrong, and wrong to be right. And so His Majesty, who had an excellent understanding, and sought after the truth, but was surrounded by low irreligious persons, to whom he gave his confidence, was plunged into scepticism. Doubt accumulated upon doubt, and the object of his search was lost. The ramparts of the law and of the true faith were broken down; and, in the course of five or six years, not one trace of Islam was left in him. The state of affairs was changed.

There were many reasons for this. But as "small things are suggestive of great ones, and fear betrays the culprit," I will only mention a few. Learned men of various kinds and from every country, and professors of many different religions and creeds, assembled at his Court, and were admitted to converse with him. [44]Night and day people did nothing but inquire and investigate. Profound points of science, the subtleties of revelation, the curistities of history, the wonders of nature, of which large volumes could only give a summary abstract, were ever spoken of. His Majesty collected the opinions of every one, especially of such as were not Muhammadans, retaining whatever he approved of, and rejecting every thing which was against his disposition, and ran counter to his wishes. From his earliest child-

[44]*The rest of this Extract is taken from Blochmann's translation. See Ain-i Akbari, vol. i. p.* 179.

hood to his manhood, and from his manhood to old age, His Majesty has passed through the most diverse phases, and through all sorts of religious practices and sectarian beliefs, and has collected everything which people can find in books, with a talent of selection peculiar to him, and a spirit of inquiry opposed to every (Islamitic) principle. Thus a faith, based on some elementary principles, traced itself on the mirror of his heart, and, as the result of all the influences which were brought to bear on His Majesty, there grew, gradually as the outline on a stone, the conviction in his heart that there were sensible men in all religions, and abstemious thinkers, and men endowed with miraculous powers, among all nations. If some true knowledge was thus everywhere to be found, why should truth be confined to one religion, or to a creed like Islam, which was comparatively new, and scarcely a thousand years old? Why should one sect assert what another denies, and why should one claim a preference without having superiority conferred on itself?

Moreover, Samanis[45] and Brahmans managed to get frequent private interviews with His Majesty. As they surpass other learned men in their treatises on morals, and on physical and religious sciences, and reach a high degree in their knowledge of the future, in spiritual power and human perfection, they brought proofs, based on reason and testimony, for the truth of their own, and the fallacies of other religions, and inculcated their doctrines so firmly, and so skilfully represented things as quite self-evident which require consideration, that no man, by expressing his doubts, could now raise a doubt in His Majesty, even if mountains were to crumble to dust, or the heavens were to tear asunder.

Hence His Majesty cast aside the Islamitic revelations regarding resurrection, the Day of Judgement, and

[45]*Hindu ascetics, Sans. Sramana.—Ed.*

the details connected with it, as also all ordinances based on the tradition of our Prophet. He listened to every abuse which the courtiers heaped on our glorious and pure faith, which can be so easily followed; and eagerly seizing such opportunities, he showed, in words and gestures, his satisfaction at the treatment which his original religion received at their hands.

CHRISTIAN MISSIONARIES

(Text, vol. ii. p. 260.) In A.H. 986 the missionries of Europe, who are called Padris, and whose chief Pontiff, called Papa (Pope), promulgates his interpretations for the use of the people, and who issues mandates that even kings dare not disobey, brought their Gospel to the King's notice, advanced proofs of the Trinity, and affirmed the truth and spread abroad the knowledges of the religion of Jesus. The King ordered Prince Murad to learn a few lessons from the Gospel, and to treat it with all due respect, and Shaikh Abu-l Fazl was directed to translate it. Instead of the inceptive "Bismillah," the following ejaculation was enjoined: "In nomine Jesu Christi,"[46] that is, "Oh! thou whose name is merciful and bountiful." Shaikh Faizi added to this, "Praise be to God! there is no one like thee—thou art he!" The attributes of the abhorred Anti-Christ were ascribed to our holy Prophet by these lying impostors.

[46]*The original has in Persian "ay nami wai zhuzhu karstu", which can scarcely be said to bear any meaning. Besides, the translation, vile as it is, shows that a foreign language must have been dealt with. It is not difficult to make "in nomine" out of the first two Persian words. (The above are the words of the printed text, but Blochmann slightly modifies and improves them, "Ai nam i tu Jesus o Kristo," "O thou whose names are Jesus and Christ."—Ain-i Akbari, vol. i. p.* 183.

WORSHIP OF THE SUN

(Text, vol. ii. p. 260.) The accursed Birbal[47] tried to persuade the King, that since the sun gives light to all, and ripens all grain, fruits and products of the earth, and supports the life of mankind, that luminary should be the object of worship and veneration; that the face should be turned towards the rising, not towards the seeting sun; that man should venerate fire, water, stones and trees, and all natural objects, even down to cows and their dung; that he should adopt the frontal mark and the Brahminical cord. Several wise men at Court confirmed what he said, by representing that the sun was the chief light of the world, and the benefactor of its inhabitants, that it was a friend to kings, and that kings established periods and eras in conformity with its motions.[48] This was the cause of the worship paid to the sun on the *Nau-roz Jalali,* and of his being induced to adopt that festival for the celebration of his accession

[47] *This is the epithet by which he is usually characterized by this bitter enemy. Respecting his death in the Yusufzai country, he says, "Birbal fled for fear of his life, and being slain, was included amongst the dogs of hell, and met with punishment, slight when compared with his evil deserts. Akbar regretted his loss more than that of any other of his chiefs, exclaiming, 'Why did they not, at least, rescue his body, that it might have been burnt?' Afterwards, he derived consolation from reflecting, that as Birbal was pure and undefiled, the rays of the grand luminary were sufficient for his funeral pyre."*

[48] *The printed text says only "padshahan marwaj uiand"—"Kings are sustained by it."—Blochmann's translation runs, "They said, the sun was 'the greatest light,' the source of benefit for the whole world, the nourisher of kings, and the origin of royal power."—Ain-i Akbari, vol. i. p.* 183.

to the throne. Every day be used to put on clothes of that particular colour which accords with that of the regent-planet of the day. He began also, at midnight and at early dawn, to mutter the spells, which the Hindus taught him, for the purpose of subduing the sun to his wishes. He prohibited the slaughter of cows, and the eating of their flesh, because the Hindus devoutly worship them, and esteem their dung as pure. Instead of cows, they sacrifice good men. The reason was also assigned, that physicians have represented their flesh to be productive of sundry kinds of sickness, and to be difficult of digestion.

ABU-L FAZL APPOINTED SUPERINTENDENT OF FIRE-TEMPLES

(Text, vol. ii. p. 261.) Fire-worshippers also came from Nausari in Gujarat, proclaimed the religion of Zardusht as the true one, and declared reverence to fire to be superior to every other kind of worship. They also attracted the King's regard, and taught him the peculiar terms, the ordinances, the rites and ceremonies of the Kaianians; and at last he directed that the sacred fire should be made over to the charge of Abu-l Fazl, and that after the manner of the Kings of Persia, in whose temples blazed perpetual fires, he should take care it was never extinguished either by night or day,—for that it is one of the signs of God, and one light from among the many lights of his creation.

From his earliest youth, in compliment to his wives, the daughters of the Rajas of Hind, he had within the female apartments continued to burn the *hom,* which is a ceremony derived from fire-worship; but on the New-year festival of the 25th year after his accession, he prostrated himself both before the sun and before the fire in public, and in the evening the whole Court had to rise up respectfully when the lamps and candles were lighted.

On the festival of the eighth day after the sun's entering Virgo in this year, he came forth to the public audience-chamber with his forehead marked like a Hindu, and he had jewelled strings tied on his wrist by Brahmans, by way of a blessing. The chiefs and nobles adopted the same practice in imitation of him, and presented on that day pearls and precious stones, suitable to their respective wealth and station. It became the current custom also to wear the *rakhi* on the wrist, which means an amulet formed out of twisted linen rags. In defiance and contempt of the true faith, every precept which was enjoined by the doctors of other religions, he treated as manifest and decisive. Those of Islam, on the contrary, were esteemed follies, innovations, inventions of indigent beggars, of rebels, and of highway robbers, and those who professed that religion were set down as contemptible idiots. These sentiments had been long growing up in his mind, and ripened gradually into a firm conviction of their truth.

INFALLIBILITY OF THE EMPEROR[49]

(Text, vol. ii. p. 270.) In the same year (987), a declaration made its appearance, which bore the signatures and seals of Makhdumu-l Mulk, Shaikh 'Abdu-n Nabi *Sadru-s Sudur*, Kazi Jalalu-d din Multani, who was *Kaziu-l Kuzat*, of Sadr-i Jahan, the *mufti* general, of Shaikh Mubarak, the most learned man of the age, and of Ghazi Khan Badakhshi, who had no rival in the scince of metaphysics. The object of this declaration was to establish the complete superiority of the *Imam-i 'adil* (just leader) over the *Mujtahid* (chief lawyer); and to make his judgement and choice a preponderating authority on divers questions, so that no one could possibly reject (his) commands, either in religious or political matters, but must by them be self-convinced.[50] . . . . I copy the document verbatim.

[49]*See Blochmann's Translation, Ain-i Akbari, vol. i. p.* 185.

[50]*This is a somewhat difficult passage. My render-*

(*Preamble—Citations from the Kuran and the Traditions.*) "We have agreed and do decree that the rank of a *Sultan-i 'adil* (just ruler) is higher in the eyes of God than the rank of *Mujtahid.* Further we declare that the Sultan of Islam, the refuge of mankind, the leader of the faithful, the shadow of God in the world—Abu-l Fath Jalalu-d din Muhammad Akbar Padshah-i Ghazi (whose kingdom God perpetuate!)—is a most just, wise, and God-fearing King. Therefore, if there be a variance of opinion among the *mujtahid* upon questions of religion, and His Majesty, in his penetrating understanding and unerring judgement, should incline to one opinion, and give his decree for the benefit of mankind and for the due regulation of the world, we do hereby agree that such a decree is binding on us and on the whole nation. Further we declare that should His Majesty, in his unerring judgement, issue an order, which is not in opposition to the Kuran, and which is for the benefit of the nation, it shall be binding and imperative on every man. Opposition to it shall involve damnation in the world to come and loss of religion and property in this life. This document has been written with honest intentions, for the glory of God, and the propagation of Islam, and is signed by us, the principal *'ulama* and lawyers, in the month of Rajab, 987 Hijra."

ing differs materially from Blochmann's; but though I have ventured to disagree with him, I have so much respect for his authority, that I subjoin his version. "The object of the document was to settle the superiority of the Imam-i 'adil (just leader) over the "Majtahid," which was proved by a reference to an ill-supported authority. The whole matter is a question, regarding which people differ in opinion; but the document was to do away with the possibility of disagreeing about laws, whether political or religious, and was to bind the lawyers in spite of themselves."

The draft of this document was in the handwriting of Shaikh Mubarak. The others had signed it against their will. But the Shaikh of his own accord added at the bottom that he had most willingly signed his name, for it was a matter which for several years he had been anxiously looking forward to.

After His Majesty had obtained this legal opinion, the road of deciding religious questions was opened, the superiority of the judgement of the *Imam* was established, and opposition was rendered impossible. The legal distinction between lawful and unlawful was set aside, the judgement of the *Imam* became paramount over the dogmas of the law, and Islam was called *Taklid* (counterfeit) . . . . His Majesty had now determined publicly to use the formula, "There is no God but God, and Akbar is God's representative." But as he found that the extravagance of this led to commotions, he restricted the use of it to a few people in the *harem*.

EXPERIMENTAL SECLUSION OF INFANTS

(Text, vol. ii. p. 288.) In this year (989 H.), in order to verify the circumstances of the case (of the man who heard without ears), an order was issued that several suckling infants should be kept in a secluded place far from habitations, where they should not hear a word spoken. Well-disciplined nurses were to be placed over them, who were to refrain from giving them any instruction in speaking, so as to test the accuracy of the tradition which says, "Every one that is born is born with an inclination to religion," by ascertaining what religion and sect these infants would incline to, and above all what creed they would repeat. To carry out this order, about twenty sucklings were taken from their mothers from a consideration in money, and were placed in an empty house, which got the name of Dumb-house. After three or four years the children all came out dumb, excepting some who died there—thus justifying the name which had been given to the house.

FRIENDEHIP OF THE AUTHOR OF THE TABAKAT-I AKBARI

(Text, vol. ii. p. 296.) One day when near Kabul, the Emperor directed the *Sadr-i Jahan* to make out and present to him a list of the pensioners (*ahl-i sa'adat*) who were present with the army, and another of those who were absent. When my (the author's) name came up, the late Khwaja Nizamu-d din Ahmad, the author of the *Tarikh-i Nizami,* with whom I had become acquainted about a year before that time, but who was as friendly as if I had known him a hundred years, in the great kindness and consideration which he showed to all his friends, and to me in particular, caused me to be put down and returned as sick.

INNOVATIONS[51]

(Text, vol. ii. p. 301.) His Majesty was now (990 H.) firmly convinced that a period of 1000 years from the mission of the Prophet was the extent of the duration of the religion of Islam, and that period was now accomplished. No obstacle remained to promulgating the designs which he secretly held. He was now free from the respect and reverence due to the *shaikhs* and *'ulama,* and from the deference owing to their authority. To his entire satisfaction, he was able to carry out his project of overturning the dogmas and principles of Islam, to set up his novel, absurd, and dangerous regulations, and to give currency to his own vicious belief.

The first order which he issued was, that the "Era of the Thousand" should be used upon the coins, and that a *Tarikh-i Alfi,* or history of the thousand years, from the *rihlat,* or death of the Prophet, should be written. Other extraordinary innovations were devised as political

[51]*See Ain-i Akbari, vol. i. p.* 191.

expedients, and such strange orders were given that men's minds got quite perplexed. . . . . Wine was allowed, if required, for strengathening the body, and if prescribed by doctors; but that no strifie and disturbance might arise, severe punishments were prescribed for drunkenness, carousals, and rows. For the sake of proper surveillance, His Majesty established a wine-shop near the palace, and put the wife of the porter in charge of it, because she belonged to the wine-selling class. The price of wine was fixed by regulations, and any sick person could obtain wine on having his own name and that of his father and grandfather written down by the clerk of the shop. Of course, people got fictitious names put down, and obtained supplies of wine. It was, in fact, nothing else but a licensed shop for drunkards. Some people even said that pork was used in the manufacture of the wine (but God knows!). Notwithstanding all restrictions, much mischief and trouble arose, and though many people were punished every day, there was no sufficient check. So (the result verified) the saying, "Upset, but do not spill."

The next matter was that the prostitutes of the realm, who had collected at the capital, and could scarcely be counted, so large was their number, had a separate quarter assigned to them outside the town, which was called Shaitanpura or Devilsville. A keeper, a deputy (*darogha*), and a clerk also were appointed over it, to write down the names of those who resorted to prostitutes, or who took them to their houses. People might indulge in such connexions, provided the toll collectors were cognizant; but without permission no one was allowed to take dancing-girls to his house. If any well-known courtier wanted to have a virgin, the *darogha* made a statement of the fact, and got permission from the Court . . . . . Drunkenness and folly led to bloodshed, and though some persons were brought to punishment, others walked about proudly and insolently parading their delinquencies. His Majesty called some of the principle prostitutes before him in private, and asked them who had deprived them of their virginity. After getting the names, some of the most renowned and trusty grandees were punished and condemned, and many of them were kept for a long time in confinement.

Another matter was the interdiction of beef, and the declaration of its being defiling. The reason of this was, that from his youth His Majesty had associated with Hindu libertines, and had thus got implanted in his heart a reverence for the cow, which, in their opinion, is a cause of the preservation of the world. The daughters of the great Rajas of Hind, of whom he had several in his *harem*, obtained such an ascendancy over him as to make him abstain from eating beef, garlic, or onions, and from associating with men who wore beards and such like persons.

DECLARATION OF ADHERENCE TO THE DIVINE FAITH[52]

(Text, vol. ii. p. 304.) Ten or twelve years after the commencement of these changes, matters came to such a pitch that wretches like Mirza Jani, chief of Tatta, and other apostates, wrote their declarations to the following effect: "I, so and so, son of so and so, have willingly and cheerfully renounced the false and pretended religion of Islam, which I have received from my ancestors, and have joined the Divine Faith (*Din-i Ilahi*) of Shah Akbar, and have assented to its fourfold rule of sincerity —(the readiness to) sacrifice wealth and life, honour and religion." These writings—there could be no more effectual letters of damnation—were handed into the *Mujtahid* of the new creed (Abu-l Fazl).

(p. 325.) His Majesty gave his religious system the name of *Tauhid-i Ilahi, Divine Monotheism.*

[52]*See Ain-i Akbari, vol. i. p.* 194.

WEALTH OF MAKHDUMU-L MULK

(Text, vol. ii. p. 311.) Makhdumu-l Mulk died at Ahmadabad, and in the year 990 Kazi 'Ali was sent from Fathpur to ascertain what property he had left. When he came to Lahore, he found such vast treasures as defied the key of conjecture to open their lock. Several chests of ingots[53] of gold were discovered in his sepulchre, where he had caused them to be buried as corpses. And the wealth which lay open to the eyes of the world was such that none but the Creator could ascertain it. All these bricks of gold, together with his books, which he looked upon as bricks, were placed in the public treasury. His sons several times underwent torture, and fell into abject poverty.

TRANSLATION OF THE MAHABHARATA

(Text, vol. ii. p. 320.) In the year 990 His Majesty assembled some learned Hindus, and gave them directions to write an explanation of the *Mahabharata*, and for several nights he himself devoted his attention to explain the meaning to Nakib Khan, so that the Khan might sketch out the gist of it in Persian. On a third night, the King sent for me, and desired me to translate the *Mahabharata*, in conjunction with Nakib Khan. The consequence was that in three or four months I translated two out of the eighteen sections, at the puerile absurdities of which the eighteen thousand creations may well be amazed. Such injunctions as one never heard of—what not to eat, and a prohibition against turnips! But such is my fate, to be employed on such works. Nevertheless, I console myself with the reflection, that what is predestined must come to pass!

After this, Mulla Shi and Nakib Khan together accomplished a portion, and another was completed by Sultan Haji Thanesari by himself. Shaikh Faizi was

[53]*khisht, lit. "bricks".*

then directed to convert the rough translation into elegant prose and verse, but he did not complete more than two sections. The Haji aforesaid again wrote it,[54] correcting the errors which had appeared in his first translation, and settling the conjectures which he had hazarded. He had revised a hundred sheets, and, nothing being omitted, he was about to give the finishing touch, when the order was received for his dismissal, and he was sent to Bakar. He now resides in his own city (Thanesar). Most of the scholars who were employed upon this translation are now with the Kauravas and Pandavas. May those who survive be saved by the mercy of God, and may their repentance be accepted!

The translation was called *Razm-nama,* and when fairly engrossed and embellished with pictures, the nobles had orders to take copies, with the blessing and favour of God. Shaikh Abu-l Fazl, who had already written against our religion, wrote the Preface, extending to two sheets. God defend us from his infidelities and absurdities!

HOUSES OF CHARITY

(Text, vol. ii. p. 324.) In A.H. 991 the King erected two buildings outside the city where he might feed *fakirs,* both Musulman and Hindu; one he called *Khairpura,* the other *Dharmpura.* Some of Abu-l Fazl's people had the charge, and used to spend the King's money in procuring food. As the *jogis* also used to flock there in great numbers, a separate receiving house was built for them, and called *Jogipura.* Nightly meetings were held in private with some of these men, and they used to employ themselves in various follies and extravagancies, in contemplations, gestures, addresses, abstractions and reveries,

[54]*The printed text of the Bibl. Ind. says "do pardah," "two portions;" but there is no such limit in the text printed with the first edition of this work.*

and in alchemy, fascination and magic. The King himself studied alchemy, and used to exhibit the gold which he made. One night in the year, called *Shiv-rat,* was appointed for a grand assembly of *jogis* from all parts of the country, on which occasion he would eat and drink with the best of them; and used to be gratified by their assurances of a life three or four times longer than the natural life of man.

RAM CHAND BHATH

(Text, vol. ii. p. 335.) The Emperor stayed four months at Allahabad, and from thence he sent Zain Khan Koka and Birbal, who was formerly in the service of Raja Ram Chand Bhath, on an embassy to Chauragarh. Ram Chand consented to do homage, and after attending to the duties of hospitality he detained Zain Khan, and proceeded along with him to Fathpur, to wait upon the Emperor. He presented a most valuable tribute of one hundred rubies and other precious stones. The value of one of the rubies exceeded 50,000 rupees. He left his son Babu in attendance on His Majesty, but the young man soon obtained leave to return home. Soon afterwards he went to his last home in the hottest hell. This Ram Chand has left no equal behind him for princely generosity. Among his other gifts, he gave a *kror* of gold (*kror zar*) to the minstrel Mian Tan Sen in one day. The Mian did not wish to leave the Raja, but a guardsman was sent to bring him back.

TRANSLATION OF THE RAMAYANA

(Text, vol. ii. p. 336.) In this year the King commanded me to make a translation of the *Ramayana,* a composition superior to the *Mahabharata.* It contains 25,000 *shloks,* and each *shlok* is a verse of sixty-five letters. The hero of its story is Ram Chand, King of the city of Audh, who is also called Ram, and whom the Hindus worship as a god in human form.

(Text, vol. ii. p. 366.) In the month of Jumada-l awwal A.H. 999, I completed the translation of the *Ramayana,* having occupied four years in the work. When I presented the book, it was greatly praised.

ANNIVERSARY OF THE CORONATION

(Text, vol. ii. p. 342.) In A. H. 993 the King held the festival of the anniversary of his coronation, according to the practice established in olden time, during which the King received entertainment from every shopkeeper,[55] and appropriate presents from the nobles, so that even food, scents, and the profits of dancers and fiddlers were carried away into the treasury. From a *mansabdar* of 5000 to a humble footman, all had to present offerings; and even I, this powerless atom, who was held in no account at all, except that I used to be styled *hazari,* from holding 1000 *bighas* rent-free, and was accustomed to liken myself to the old woman in the story of Joseph (God's blessing on him!), had to present my forty rupees, which received the honour of being accepted. I do not like my position, and should be glad to be in any other!

During this festival, the King's eldest son received a *mansab* of 12000; the second, one of 9000; and the third, one of 7000.

RAJA TODAR MAL

(Text, vol. ii. p. 365.) Thirty-third Year. Kalij Khan now returned from Gujarat, bringing various offerings, and an order was issued associating him with Raja Todar

[55]*The words are—"har ruz mihmani har dukandari az omra u peshkash layak mi giriftand." So that the contributions from the shops were presented by the nobles. In a similar passage relating to the year* 991 *it is said that the shops were regularly allotted to the nobles "bidastur sabeq dukanhara bar umra taqsim namuda."*

Mal in the administration of the Civil and Revenue Business. The Raja was now grown feeble and senile, and one night an enemy in ambush inflicted a superficial wound upon him with a sword.

THE AUTHOR'S LANDS

(Text, vol. ii. p. 368.) In A.H. 996 the King called to mind something about the book which I was then translating, and directed Hakim Abu-l Fath to give me a horse, a shawl, and some other presents. He then observed to Shah Fathu-lla 'Azdu-d daulah, that the whole of Basawar had been granted to him in *jagir,* with all its *ayma* land, and that as I, a native of Badaun, had thus lost my *madad-m'ash* land, His Majesty had conferred upon me some of equal value in Badaun, in lieu of it. Shah Fathu-lla then presented in a bag an offering of 1000 rupees, which, by exactions and other most oppressive means, his agents had recovered from the wretched widows and orphans of Basawar; and upon his representing that his officers had collected this surplus from the *ayma* lands (fraudulently alienated from the public rent-roll), the King told him to retain the money for himself. Three months after this the Shah died, and when my *farman* was engrossed, I took leave for a year, went first to Basawar, and then to Badaun, from which place I wished to make a journey to Gujarat, to see Mirza Nizamu-d din Ahmad, but delays occurred to prevent my carrying this intention into effect.

RAJA OF KUMAUN

(Text, vol. ii. p. 365.) In A.H. 996, the Raja of Kumaun arrived at Lahore from the Siwalik hills, for the purpose of paying his respects. Neither he nor his ancestors (the curse of God on them!) could ever have expected to speak face to face with an Emperor. He brought several rare presents, and amongst them a Tibet cow and a musk-deer, which latter died on the road from the effect of the heat. I saw it with my own eyes, and it had the appearance of a fox. Two small tusks projected from the mouth, and, instead of horns, it had a slight elevation, or bump. As the hind quarters of the animal were enveloped in a cloth, I could not examine the whole body. They said that there were men in those hills, who had feathers and wings, and who could fly, and they spoke of a mango-tree in that country which yields fruit all the year round. God knows whether this is true!

THE EMPEROR'S ILLNESS

(Text, vol. ii. p. 376.) In this year the Emperor was somewhat indisposed. He had pains in his stomach, and other disturbances which no one could account for. Through this inability to understand his ailment, suspicions arising from malevolence were cast upon the eldest prince, and whispers of poison flew about.

THE COINAGE

(Text, vol. ii. p. 380.) Among the edicts issued (in the thirty-seventh year of the reign), was one that all the *dirhams* and *dinars* bearing the devices of former kings should be melted and sold for the price of the gold and silver, so that not a trace of them should remain in the world. The various *ashrafis* and rupees of the Emperor's coinage, whether old or recent, were at once to be put in circulation, and no difference whatever between them and the old coins was to be recognized. Kalij Khan endeavoured to enforce this order. *Sarrafs* were every day called up; bonds were taken from them, and fines were inflicted on them. As a last resource, some were put to death. But for all this they did not refrain from counterfeiting the coin (*kallabi*). Orders and instructions upon this subject were written and sent to the most remote parts of the dominions, but without effect, until Khwaja Shamsu-d din Khwafi, the *diwan*, succeeded in putting all these orders in force.

SHAIKH 'ABDU-N NABI

(Text, vol. iii. p. 79.) Shaikh 'Abdu-n Nabi, *Sadru-s Sudur*, was son of Shaikh Ahmad, son of Shaikh Abdu-l Kudus, of Gangoh. He went several times to Mecca and Medina, and studied the traditions. . . . . He put on the appearance of great piety. When he was appointed to the *Sadarat*, he distributed among the people an immense quantity of *madad-m'ash*, *wakf*, and pensions. No *Sadr* during any former reign had so much power, and no one gave away one-tenth of the *wakf* which he did.[56] The

[56]*It is quite impossible to reconcile this eulogy with the taunting and acrimonious tone adopted elsewhere; nor does any conceivable variety in the reading of the two texts admit of any essential difference of sentiment; unless, indeed, we consider that the grasping Sadr was Makhdumu-l Mulk, and not Shaikh 'Abdu-n Nabi; which appears opposed to the whole tenor of the text, and especially to 'Abdu-n Nabi's declaration at the close of the Extract. It is scarcely permitted us to imagine that so grave an author might possibly be indulging in a little playful irony.*

The duties and responsibilities of the Sadr resembled those of a Chancellor, or an Ecclesiastical Registrar, the chief difference being, that when the Sadr, as we have seen to be frequently the case, plundered the property of helpless widows and orphans, he was flayed alive, or trodden to death by elephants. As such punishments would be esteemed barbarous in modern times, and as our tortuous system of law generally delights to exercise its sophistries and subtilties in behalf of notorious criminals, there can be little doubt that, if any Sadr were in these days to prostitute the sacred obligations of his office to such infernal purposes,, he would escape with impunity:—at leaset upon earth.

Committunt eadem diverso crimina fato;
Ille crucem pretium sceleris tulit, hic diadema.

King was for some time so intimate and unceremonious with him, that he would rise to adjust the Shaikh's slippers when he took his leave. At last, through the enmity of Makhdumu-l Mulk and some other ill-disposed and deceitful doctors, he fell in the King's estimation, and began to be treated very differently. The chief reason of the change was this:

At the time that the King arrived at Fathpur from Banswara, Kazi 'Abdu-r Rahim, of Muttra, complained to the Shaikh that a rich and obstinate Brahman had taken all the materials, which he had collected for the building of a mosque, and applied them to his own purposes in building a temple for an idol, and that when he remonstrated with him, the Brahman, in the presence of a multitude of people (may his mouth be crammed with mud!), applied foul and abusive language to the Prophet (the peace of God rest with him!), and grossly reviled all Musulmans. When the Brahman was summoned before the Shaikh, he refused to come, so Shaikh Abu-l Fazl was sent to bring him. Shaikh Abu-l Fazl on his return represented what he had heard from the people of Muttra; namely, that the Brahman certainly had used foul language. Upon this, the learned in the law decided, some of them for death, some for public exposure and fine. They were consequently divided into two parties, and disputed at great length on the subject. Although the Shaikh went to ask for leave to punish him capitally, the King would give no distinct reply, but said vaguely, that the Shaikh was himself responsible for carrying into execution the sentence of the law, and inquired why he consulted him. During this long suspense the Brahman continued in prison, and notwithstanding that the ladies of the royal household used their exertions to get him released, yet out of regard to the Shaikh, the King would not give his consent.

The Shaikh continued to importune the King for a reply, but all he could get was, that he had already expressed his opinion, and the Shaikh knew what it was. When the Shaikh returned to his home, he immediately issued orders for the Brahman's death. When the King learnt this, he was very angry. The ladies within, and the Hindus without, the palace, exclaimed, "Is this the man whom you have promoted and favoured, and has he reached to such a pitch of insolence as not to regard your wishes, and to put a man to death for the mere purpose of displaying his power and authority?" They continued to pour such-like complaints into the ears of the King, so that he could no longer endure them. . . . . One night, at Anup-talao, a conclave of divines assembled, from whom he inquired their opinions on the subject. . . . . The King at last singled me out, and said, "When ninety and nine opinions are in favour of a sentence of death, and a hundredth in favour of acquittal, do you think it right that the *muftis* should act upon the latter? What is your opinion?" I replied, that it was a legal maxim that punishment should not be inflicted where there was any doubt. The King was sorrowful, and said, "Was not Shaikh 'Abdu-n Nabi aware of this maxim, that he killed that unfortunate Brahman?" I replied, that the Shaikh was certainly a wise man, and that he no doubt had acted in direct contravention of the law, but that he might possibly have adopted that course for the sake of expendiency. . . . .

The King's agitation was so great that his hair stood on end, like that of a roused lion, and some people behind me whispered that I should not carry the controversy any further. All of a sudden, he turned towards me and said, "You are not at all right." Upon which I made a low bow, and retired to a little distance. From that day I have abandoned my presumptuous and controversial manner, and take my place apart from the groups which surround the throne. It is only now and then that I venture to advance, and make my obeisance at a respectful distance.

It was on this account that Shaikh 'Abdu-n Nabi's prosperity declined. . . . He died in the year 991.

SHAIKH FAIZI

(Text, vol. iii. p. 299.) Commonly called the "chief of Poets." He excelled in the arts of versification, enigmatic lines and rhyming. In history, in philology, in medicine, in letter-writting, and in composition, he was without a rival. His earlier compositions in verse bear his titular name of Faizi, which he subsequently dignified into Faiyazi, in order that it might correspond with the grammatical amplification of 'Allami, by which his younger brother, Abu-l Fazl, was known; but the change was ill-omened, for he survived to enjoy his last title only one or two months, and then met his death with great alarm and inquietude.

As an author, he was sometimes serious, sometimes jocose, conceited, proud, and malevolent. He was full of hypocrisy, malignity, dissimulation, ambition, arrogance, and egotism. In his obstinacy and animosity he reviled the earlier and later *Khalifas* and disciples, the ancestors and descendants of the Prophet, the wise and the excellent, the pious and the saintly, and, in short, all Musulmans in general, and ridiculed the principles of their faith, privately and publicly, by night and by day. His conduct was so abominable, that even Jews, Christians, Hindus, Sabians, and Guebres are considered a thousand times less odious. He acted entirely against the tenets of the Muhammadan religion. What was forbidden in that, was lawful to him, and *vice versa*.

He composed a commentary upon the Kuran, consisting entirely of letters without diacritical points, in order to obliterate his infamy, but the waters of a hundred oceans will never cleanse the stain he has contracted, until the day of judgement. He composed it in the very height of his drunkenness and impurity, and dogs were allowed to tread on every letter of it. In the same spirit of pride, stubbornness, and infidelity, he met his final doom, and in a manner which I trust no one may again see, or hear of; for when the King paid him a visit on his death-bed, he barked at his face like a dog, as the King himself acknowledged in public; his whole face was swollen, and his lips appeared black, insomuch that the King observed to Abu-l Fazl, "What is this blackness? Surely the Shaikh has been rubbing dentifrice on his teeth, according to the Indian fashion?" "No," replied Abu-l Fazl, "it is the stain of the blood which he has been spitting."[57] In truth, even this scene was but a small retribution for the blasphemies of which he had been guilty, and for the contumelies which he had uttered against the Prophet, the last of the apostles (the peace of God be upon him, and all his family!). Several abusive chronograms were written on the occasion, of which the following are only a few. . . . .

He had composed poetry for forty years, correct enough in point of versification and language, but utterly destitute of beauty, either in sentiment or religion.[58] He has joined the dry bones together pretty well, but the skeleton has no brains. The condiments of verse are sufficiently abundant, but quite tasteless, ... as is proved by no one remembering his lines, although the very vilest poets meet with some quoters and admirers. Nevetheless, he wrote, what with *diwans* and *masnavis*,

[57]*At the close of the historical narrative, the author tells us that Faizi had been spitting blood for six months before his death, and that his barking like a dog was the consequence of his making those animals his constant companions night and day, to insult the Musulmans, to whom they are an abomination.*

[58]*This is by no means the general estimate of his poetry, which is greatly admired in India, even to this day. The sense of the text is accurately preserved here, but the translation is somewhat amplified.—Ed.*

more than twenty thousand lines, and, notwithstanding that he expended the rich revenues of his *jagir* upon their transcription, and in sending copies to his friends, far and near, not one of them ever read his poems twice. The following verses of his own selection were given by him to Nizamu-d din Ahmad and others, as a memento. . . . . . Pray tell me what beauty there is in them!

At the time that Shaikh Faizi had gone to take charge of his office of the duputyship of the Dakhin, I wrote him two letters from the foot of the Kashmir hills, and informed him of the cause of the King's displeasure and his refusal to allow me to pay my respects. Upon this he wrote to the King a letter of recommendation, which was cauched in the following words, and despatched it, on the 10th of Jumada-l awwal, A.H. 1000, from Ahmadnagar to Lahore, and orders were given to Abu-l Fazl to place it in the *Akbar-nama,* so that it might be generally read.

"May it please Your Majesty! Two friends of Mulla 'Abdu-l Kadir have arrived from Badaun in great distress and sorrow, representing that the Mulla has been for some time ill, and that in consequence of his failing to perform the promise which he made respecting his return, the servants of the government have treated him with great severity, and that there is no knowing what the result of it may be. They inquired also if the prolonged illness of the Mulla was known to Your Majesty.

"Healer of the broken-hearted! Mulla Abdu-l Kadir is a very able man, and is well acquainted with all the sciences usually cultivated by the Mullas of Hindustan, and he was also a pupil of my father's. Your slave has been acquainted with him for nearly thirty-seven years. Besides being a person of deep learning, he is a poet, and composes elegantly in Arabic and Persian. He is not a mere imitator, but an original thinker. He also knows a little of Hindu astrology and accounts, and is not at a loss in any field of knowledge. He is acquainted with a foreign, as well as with Indian music, and can play at both the small and big games of chess; moreover, he writes a pretty good hand. Notwithstanding that he possesses all these accomplishments, he is content and entirely divested of avarice, of equable temperament, and a person of excellent morals and manners, but poor, and with no fixed income. He is sincere and warm-hearted, and has every confidence in Your Majesty's kindness.

"At the time that the army was before Kombhalmir, he volunteered to join it. There he did the State good service, and received a donation for his wounds. Jalal Khan Korchi, when he first introduced him at Court, said, 'I have brought a preacher to present to Your Majesty, that Your Majesty may be gratified.' Mir Fathu-lla also represented something respecting the Mulla's circumstances, and my worthy brother, Abu-l Fazl, also knows him well. But according to the proverb, 'A grain of good luck is better than a sack full of skill.'

"As the Court is the abode of the virtuous, I have taken the liberty to bring this destitute person to notice, and to place him before the foot of the throne, as if I was myself present. Did I not advocate his claims at this time, I should consider myself guilty of an offence against the cause of truth and justice.

"May God, the omnipotent, place the slaves of the Court under the heavenly shadow of your royal Majesty! and may he mercifully make their feet firm in pursuing the path of rectitude and justice, and in acquiring the knowledge of truth! May he preserve Your Majesty as the protector and nourisher of the helpless, the bestower of mercy, the pardoner of errors, throughout the world and all worlds, and bless you with thousands upon thousands of sources of wealth, abundance, grandeur and felicity, upon earth and in heaven! I implore all this for the sake of the pure spirits who surround the throne of grace, and the saints upon earth who join in the matutinal chorus of prayer. Amen, Amen, Amen."

Should any one, upon perusing this, observe, that Shaikh Faizi's regard and affection for me, which is evidenced by this letter, is but ill requited by the harshness and severity with which I have spoken of him, especially after his death, when the precept of "speak not ill of the dead" should be strictly observed, I have only to reply, that the observation is perfectly just, but under the circumstances, I inquire, what could I do? seeing that the truth of religion and the maintenance of one's faith are paramount to all other obligations, and that the maxim I never divite from is, that my love and hatred should be subservient to God's cause. Although I was Shaikh Faizi's companion for forty years, nevertheless, after he apostatized from his religion, changed his manners, and entered on vain controversies, I became gradually estranged from him, and, especially after what occurred at his death, I hold myself no longer his friend. When we are all summoned before the throne of God, we shall receive sentence according to our deserts!

Shaikh Faizi left a library of 4600 volumes, some of them exquisitely copied with, what may be said to be, even unnecessary care and expense. Most of them were autographs of the respective authors, or at least copied by their contemporaries. They were all transferred to the King's Library, after being catalogued and numbered in three different sections. The first included Poetry, Medicine, Astrology, and Music; the second, Philosophy, Sufyism, Astronomy, and Geometry; and the third or lowest grade, included Commentaries, Traditions, Theology, and Law. There were also 101 different copies of his poem, *Nal-Daman*.

WAKI'AT

OF

SHAIKH FAIZI

[BUT for the great name of the writer, this little work would scarcely deserve notice. It consists of a series of letters written to the Emperor by Shaikh Faizi, while he was absent on his embassy to the Dakhin, in the thirty-sixth year of the reign. The letters are of a gossiping familiar character, and are embellished with plenty of verses; but they contain nothing of importance, and throw little light upon the political relations of the time.

All these letters were translated for Sir H. M. Elliot by Lieut. Prichard, and it is to be regretted that they were not more worthy of the labour bestowed upon them.

Faizi cannot be considered an historian, so a memoir of his life would be out of place in this work. A full and satisfactory one will be found in Blochmann's *Ain-i Akbari*, vol. i. p. 490.]

EXTRACT

After travelling a long distance, and accomplishing many stages, I arrived on the 20th of the month of December (Pur), at a place fifty *kos* from Burhanpur, and the next day pitched my camp and arranged my tent in a manner befitting a servant of the Court. The tent was so arranged as to have two chambers; in the second or innermost of which, the royal throne was placed, with the gold-embroidered cushion on it: over which the canopy of velvet, worked with gold, was erected. The royal sword and the dresses of honour were placed on the throne, as well as Your Majesty's letter, whilst men were standing around with folded hands.

The horses also, that were to be given away, were standing in their proper place. Raja 'Ali Khan, accompanied by his followers, and the *vakil* and magistrate of the Dakhin, approached with that respect and reverence that betokened their obedience and good-will to Your Majesty. They dismounted some distance from the tent, and were admitted into the outer chamber. They approached respectfully, and were permitted to proceed onwards. When they entered the second chamber, and saw the royal throne at some distance from them, they saluted it, and advanced with bare feet. When they arrived at a certain distance, they were directed to stand and make three salutations, which they did most respectfully, and continued standing in the place. I then took the royal letter in both hands, and calling him a little nearer, said, "His Majesty, the vicegerent of God, has sent your highness two royal orders, with the greatest condescension and kindness,—this is one." On this, he took the letter and put it on his head respectfully, and saluted it three times. I then said, "His Majesty has bestowed on your highness a dress of honour." Upon this he bowed, kissed it, and bowed again. In the same way he did homage for the sword, and bowed every time Your Majesty's name was mentioned. He then observed, "I have for years wished to be seated in your presence," and, at the same time, he appeared anxious to do so. Whereupon I requested him to be seated, and he respectfully sat down in your humble servant's presence. When a fitting opportunity offered itself, I addressed him warily, and said I could show him how he might promote his interest; but the chief part of my discourse consisted of praises and eulogiums of Your Majesty. He replied that he was a devoted servant of Your Majesty, and considered himself highly favoured that he had seen your Majesty's good-will and favour. I replied, "His Majesty's kindness towards you is great, he looks upon you as a most intimate friend, and reckons you among his confidential servants; the greatest proof of which is, that he has sent a man of rank to you." At this he bowed several times, and seemed pleased. During this time I twice made signs that I wished the audience to close; but he said, "I am not yet satisfied with my interview, and wish to sit here till the evening." He sat there for four or five *gharis* (an hour and a half). At last the betel-leaf and scents were brought. I asked him to give them to me with his own hands. I gave him several pieces of betel with my own hands, at which he bowed several times. I then said, "Let us repeat the prayer for the eternal life and prosperity of His Majesty," which he did most respectfully, and the audience was broken up. He then went and stood respectfully in his place at the edge of the carpet opposite the throne. The royal horses were there. He kissed the reins, placed them on his shoulder, and saluted them. He then took his departure. My attendant counted and found that he made altogether twenty-five salams. He was exceedingly happy and contented. When he first came in he said, "If you command me, I am ready to make 1,000 salams in honour of His Majesty. I am ready to sacrifice my life for him." I observed, "Such conduct befits friendship and feelings such as yours, but His Majesty's orders forbid such adoration; and whenever the courtiers perform such adoration out of their feelings of devotion, His Majesty forbids them, for such acts of worship are for God alone."

WIKAYA'-I ASAD BEG

[THIS work is also called *Halat-i Asad Beg*. It is an interesting personal memoir of the author during the latter years of Akbar's reign, containing accounts of some of the political transactions of that period, especially of the murder of Abu-l Fazl.

A Persian note at the end of Sir H. M. Elliot's MS. gives the following account of the author:

"Asad Beg of Kazwin, the author of this work, was well known and noted for his kindness, magnanimity, benevolence, and great experience in business. When he first came to India, he spent a period of seventeen years in the service of Shaikh Abu-l Fazl, son of Shaikh Mubarak. After the death of Shaikh Abu-l Fazl, he was appointed an officer at the Court of His Majesty the Emperor Akbar, and obtained such distinguished employments and offices that he gained wealth and honour. In a short time the life and times of Akbar came to an end, and the reign of His Majesty Jahangir commenced. Although at first he was not admitted at Court, yet he continued a constant and good servant of the State. Towards the close of the reign of Jahangir he was honoured with the title of Peshrau Khan. He died at the commencement of the reign of His Majesty Shah Jahan in the year 1041."[1]

The whole of this work was translated for Sir H. M. Elliot by B. W. Chapman, of the Bengal Civil Service. Several Extracts have been taken from it, and the following is a general summary of its contents:

The first Extract gives the author's account of the

[1]*Asad Beg died in the third year of the reign of Jahangir and left 15 lacs of rupees behind him."—Kamgar Khan.*

death of Abu-l Fazl. Very much against his will and earnest entreaties, Asad was left behind by Abu-l Fazl at Sironj. Four days afterwards he heard of the murder of the Shaikh, and then he proceeded to fortify himself at Sironj. Soon he received a peremptory order to repair to Court. On reaching Kalabagh, he came up with Abu-l Fazl's heavy baggage, which had been left behind, and had been entrenched by the officers in charge. On reaching the scene of the disaster, he recovered a valuable casket of jewels, which a servant had preserved by hiding in the jungle. The baggage was worth four or five lacs of rupees, and he conveyed it safely to Agra.

On his arrival at Court, he found that Akbar was greatly incensed at him for supposed negligence in protecting his master, Abu-l Fazl, and he heard, with great dismay, the Emperor's command to "bring Asad into the bath-room, that I may cut him in pieces with my own hand." Upon ascertaining the facts the Emperor was appeased, and conversed freely with him. Asad then received a dress of honour, and was soon afterwards made captain of the Emperor's body-guard. He got also "an estate from the lapsed lands of the criminal Shah 'Ali Khan," from which he realized in the first year 17,000, the second 20,000, and the third 23,000 rupees.

Shortly afterwards he was sent as commissioner of inquiry to the camp of the Ray-rayan, in consequence of Abu-l Fazl's murderer, Nar Singh, having broken out of a fort in which he was besieged and made his escape. Upon reaching the camp, the officers endeavoured to secure Asad's favour by offering presents, amounting to 18,000 rupees, which he refused to take. The Ray-rayan showed him great attention, and Asad came to a decision which hushed matters up, and was satisfactory to all concerned. He says he received a horse, and some garments as a parting gift from the Ray-rayan, but refused an elephant. On his return to Court, he presented his report, which the Emperor approved, to the great joy of the inculpated officers and their friends. "This", he says, "was my first employment, and I brought it thus happily to a conclusion, so that no one got either disgrace or honour; but I obtained great praise and a handsome gratuity. . . . I immediately returned to the confidential service of the Emperor, in whose favour I rose from day to day, till at last I was appointed treasurer of the offerings, a very agreeable office."

He had held this office only a few months when the Emperor sent him on a mission to the Dakhin. Akbar, in 1009 H., had sent Mir Jamalu-d din Husain to Bijapur, to arrange a marriage between his son, Prince Daniyal, and a daughter of the King of Bijapur. Asad was now commissioned to bring back the Mir with the promised bride. This must have been in or just before the year 1013, for the marriage took place in that year. His instructions will be found among the Extracts. He received 20,000 rupees towards his expenses. On reaching Birar he was entertained by Prince Daniyal, and received from him and his nobles "nearly 100,000 rupees, fifty horses, and ten camels." On entering the Bijapur territories he was entertained by Mir Jamalu-d din and by 'Adil Khan's daughter.

Soon afterwards he reached Bijapur, and had his interview with the King, who, as he tells us, spoke Marathi, "for although he understood Persian well, he could not speak it fluently." Akbar had directed Asad to stay only one day at Bijapur. This greatly annoyed the King, who was also vexed that he had not received a direct cession of a town called Gwalior. He offered Asad 200,000 pagodas to alter his plan, and although Asad on this as on other occasions, records his superiority to a bribe, he is evidently astonished at his own moderation. "I did not", says he, "touch a coin of the 200,000 pagodas, a sum equal to 600,000 rupees." Mir Jamal blamed him for being so scrupulous, and Asad then found out why the Mir was so reluctant to leave the Dakhin:—"he got every year three to four hundred thousand pagodas from Bijapur and Golconda."

The question of presents to the Emperor came on between the King and Asad, and gave rise to a great deal of haggling. The King asked what the Emperor had the greatest taste for, and was answered, a "rare jewels and choice elephants." An elephant and some jewels were at length presented, and Asad prepared to leave. He was offered for himself 100,000 *laris,* equal to 35,000 rupees, an elephant, horses, etc., but refused to received them. Asad wore a badge as a disciple of Akbar's "Divine religion." The King took this to examine it, and, professing himself a disciple, declared he would keep it, and Asad got it back with much trouble on a promise of obtaining one specially for the King. When he left, the King sent 9000 pagodas as a present after him. A short Extract descriptive of Bijapur has been taken from this part of the work.

The Princess and Mir Jamalu-d din accompanied him on his return; but on reaching the boundary river (Bhima?), the troops and the Princes made some demur to proceeding further. In the night a great storm of wind arose, which blew down the tents. The Bijapur escort dispersed and the Princess ran away; but in the morning she and her guardian were brought back "in great shame" by Mir Jamalu-d din. It seems evident that the Princess and her friends were averse to the match which had been arranged for her. After her return Asad continued his journey, and conducted the Princess to Ahmadnagar. He was favourably received by Prince Daniyal, who presented him with robes of honour and arms. The Prince also directed that 10,000 rupees should be given to him, but he got "only 2000 *muzaffaris.* He left Mir Jamalu-d din with the Prince, and proceeded towards Agra. He had with him the elephant which the King of Bijapur had sent to the Emperor. This animal had been accustomed to drink two *mans* of wine daily, and Asad, being unable to procure wine on his journey, was obliged to supply the animal's wants from some "chests of costly Portugal wine", which he had bought at Bijapur as a present to the Emperor.

On arriving at Court, he was very graciously received. He records how, in a fit of rage, Akbar, on the night of his arrival, ordered a wretched servant to be thrown over the battlements, and that he dismissed his chamberlain in disgrace. Asad was appointed to the vacant office, the duties of which were to introduce persons to an audience of the Emperor. This office he held for a year. He was also raised to the command of 250, and he obtained a further allowance of 17,000 rupees out of the estates of Shah 'Ali Khan. He was satisfied with his fortune, and exclaims, "What times those were, and what a blessing rested upon them!" Two Extracts have been taken from this part of the work; one giving an account of the savage execution of the servant, and the other relating to Asad's introduction of tobacco, which it appears was till then unknown at the Emperor's Court.

Asad was next appointed envoy to the four provinces of the Dakhin, with the objects stated in the Extract which follows. He was promised promotion to the rank of 1000 on his return, but this he never got. He proceeded on his mission, and, on reaching the Chanda pass, had some fighting with the men of "Raja Bhoj", who demanded the usual tolls, but Asad made his way through by night. On reaching Ujjain, he heard of the death of the Emperor. Continuing his journey, he reached Burhanpur, and there and elsewhere he records the debauchery and gambling which were prevalent among the nobles, and into which he entered with evident zest. Soon after Jahangir's accession he was recalled, and on his return he found the new monarch angry and very ill-disposed towards him. He was at once dismissed with the words, "I will not keep him,—let him go where he likes." His account of the death of

Akbar and the accession of Jahangir will be found among the Extracts.

Sir H. M. Elliot's MS. is a 32 mo. of 292 pages, thirteen lines to the page.]

EXTRACTS

Murder of Abu-l Fazl

This least of the servants of Allah, Asad, son of Muhammad Murad, has written the following: When the auspicious life of the most learned Nawab, Shaikh Abu-l Fazl, son of Shaikh Mubarak, came to a close, and that most excellent of the men of genius of his age and most rare one of his time was killed at Sarai Barar,[2] a dependency of Sironj, at prayer time on Friday, the 7th of Rabi'u-l awwal, in the year 1010, and when the news of that dire calamity and dreadful event reached that shadow of God, the Emperor Akbar, he was extremely grieved, disconsolate, distressed, and full of lamentation. That day and night he neither shaved, as usual, nor took opium, but spent his time in weeping and lamenting. It was then that the love of that Emperor of the world shone forth; for in the midst of his distressing grief and uneasiness, he thought of the author of these lines, and said to those around him, "What has become of Asad?" They, not knowing what had happened to this broken-winged one, could not answer. Just then Mirza Ja'far Asaf Khan came in, and could not refrain from weeping, on seeing his sovereign in the depths of grief and sorrow. His Lord asked him what news he had of Asad? Whether he was with Abu-l Fazl, or not? That noble chief, drying his tears, replied with courtesy, "Asad Beg was with him as far as Sironj, but the deceased Shaikh appointed him to govern the conquered provinces in Malwa, leaving with him the troops he had

[2]*Two or three stages from Sironj.*

brought from the Dakhin, while he himself, taking those which Gopal Das Nakta had enlisted in Malwa, set off for the Court. Asad was most unwilling to obey, and being much distressed, he begged permission to escort him to Gwalior: but the Shaikh would not consent, and left with his veterans at Sironj. It is pretty certain that Asad was not with him in the fight." The Emperor immediately ordered Asaf Khan instantly to write a *farman* with his own hand to Asad, ordering him to leave all the followers of the deceased Shaikh with Gopal Das at Sironj, and to come with his own people to Court as soon as possible. Asaf Khan sat down, and did as his lord directed, then sealing it with his seal, delivered it to Miyan Gada, with orders to send it by one of his own brothers to Asad at Sironj, and bring him away with his attendants.

It was decreed by the will of Providence, that the most learned should travel thus, and his fortune was perfidious; therefore it was that, following the advice of Gopal Das Nakta, he went unattended and unguarded to the place of his death, as I will now explain: When that most learned one reached the city of Sironj, the wretched villian Gopal Das had been for a long time ruler of those parts, and had raised about 300 irregular cavalry, most of them low Rajputs, who did not receive more than twenty rupees a month. Meanwhile that learned one, and we also, had heard in the Dakhin the account of Raja Nar[3] Singh Deo's depredations, and never a day passed but despatches on this subject reached us from Abu-l Khan and the rest of our faithful friends. Still, Fate so ordered it, that that learned one never paid the least heed to them. When we reached

[3]*In this MS. he is invariably called "Nar Sing," not "Bir Singh," as in the Takmila-i Akbar-nama. Blochmann also calls him "Bir Sing," but "Nar Sing" is the more likely name of the two.*

Sironj, Gopal Das persuaded him that the troops which he had brought with him from the Dakhin were many of them sick and fatigued from the speed of their march, and that it would be well to provide for them there, leaving them with Asad Beg to fight against Indrajit Bundela, and taking with him as his guard the fresh troops which he had raised.

The ill-fated learned one agreed to this unwise proposition, and throwing away his life. preferred those fresh troops, who had never faced a single enemy, to his own victorious soldiers, tried in a thousand fights. In fact, many of these men did not even arrive in time to be of any use. He had taken Gadai Khan the Afghan and his son with him, but left their troops with me; had he but had a hundred of them with him, that disastrous accident had never occurred. True, Gadai Khan was a tried courageous man, but he fought alone; he fell, charging the enemy; his son escaped with a wound. Another Afghan, Jalal Khan by name, charged and fell; and two others, Salim Khan and Sher Khan, were taken prisoners, and put to death for refusing to betray the most learned. Mansur Chabuk too, one of the Nawab Khan-khanan's servants, who had resigned his former office and come to Sironj, under pretence of turning *fakir,* and had been employed in the kitchen, charged and fell; he was of the Turkoman race. Mirza Muhammad Khan Beg was also among the slain, as well as Jabbar Khassa-khail, an Abyssinian, who was with them. When the Nawab was pierced and fell, he slew the Rajput who had wounded him, and rushed upon the enemy. He had still life in him when Nar Singh came up with the main body. He first trod Jabbar under foot, and then cut off the head of the great 'Allami. Excepting those I have mentioned, all, whether veterans or raw troops, escaped. Had they set off, as Mirza Muhsin, son-in-law of Fazl Khan of Badakhshan, advised, when he told them that robbers were lying in wait, they would have arrived safely; but as Fate had decreed, so it occurred; there was no help for it. The day when the deceased 'Allami gave me a dress of honour and a horse at Sironj, and dismissed me in the presence of Gopal Das, Mahdi 'Ali the Kashmirian, and all the attendants, with tearful eyes, I entreated to be allowed to escort him as far as Gwalior with the troops that he had left with me; but he would by no means consent, for the hour of that great man had arrived, and it was decreed that he should go. When he mounted to start, I too mounted, in order to follow him; but he peremptorily forbade me to do so, or even to come out of my house, and dismissed me from that place. . . .

When 'Allami arrived at Sarai Barar and dismounted from his horse, a religious begger came to him, and told him all particulars about Nar Singh Bundela, how he intended to attack him the next day on his march; but he only dismissed him with a present of money, such as he used to give to others of his class. That night he passed in careless security. On Friday morning he rose, and performing his ablutions, clothed himself in the white garments usually worn on Friday, and in the gold-embroidered robes of victory. He then courteously dismissed all who had attended him from the neighbouring provinces on the part of the *jagirdars* and receivers of revenue, such as the servants of Mirza Rustam, who had a *jagir* in the neighbourhood, and had sent forty or fifty horsemen, and Shaikh Mustafa, governor of Kalabagh, who had a guard with him, and several other persons of that sort, amounting in all to about 200 horsemen, who would have been of great service had he retained them. But it is in vain to lament. When Fate droops its wing from heaven, the most able men become deaf and dumb.

As the sun rose, that rising sun set off with Ya'kub Khan, with whom he was at that time very familiar. The attendants hearing the drum beat for marching, prepared to follow. The private tent of Abu-l Fazl was yet standing, when the troops of the Bundela appeared from behind the Sarai with a shout, and fell upon the camp. All the attendants who were ready, mounted and escaped along the road, while Mirza Muhsin of Badakhshan, who was in the act of mounting, got on his horse and advanced towards the robbers to reconnoitre. When he had gone a little way, he came upon Nar Singh's main body. After carefully surveying these forces from an eminence, he, like a courageous man, cut his way through them all, horse and foot, and reached 'Allami. As soon as he came up with the escort, he saw at a glance that they were all quite off their guard, marching in disorder, careless, and without their arms. Going forward, he reported what he had seen of the robbers. As soon as the Shaikh heard it, he halted and asked him what was to be done. He advised him to proceed rapidly. The Shaikh said, "You mean we are to fly?" He answered, "It is not flying; only let us go on thus," and, striking his spurs into his horse, he set forward at a rapid pace, saying, "Let us proceed in this way; as I am going, so do you go, as far as Gwalior."

While 'Allami was halting thus long, a troop of the robbers caught the elephant which bore the standard and drum, and fell upon the escort; so the fighting commenced. The Shaikh turned back, and had just reached the drum and ensign, which was at the distance of a bow-shot, when the noise of Nar Singh's army which consisted of about 500 horsemen clad in mail, was heard. Gadai Khan the Afghan, with several other armed horsemen who were on in front, charged and seizing the bridle of the Shaikh's horse, exclaimed, "What have you to do here? Do you begone! This is our business." With these words that brave soldier attacked the enemy, with his son and others before mentioned, and fell. At that moment one of the strangers in the company said, "The robbers are armed, and your attendants are not; we had better escape to the skirts of the hills; perhaps we may save our lives." So he took the bridle of the Shaikh's horse and turned about. Just then the robbers made an onslaught, spearing every man within reach. A Rajput came up and struck the Shaikh with a spear in the back, so that it came out through his breast. There was a small stream in the place, and the Shaikh tried to leap his horse over it, but he fell in the attempt. Jabbar Khassa-khail, who was close behind, slew that Rajput, and then dismounting, drew the Shaikh from under his horse and carried him a little off the road; but as the wound was mortal, the Shaikh fell.

Just then Nar Singh coming up with the rest of the Rajputs, Jabbar concealed himself behind a tree. But the horses of the Shaikh attracted the attention of Nar Singh, and he halted. The driver of the Shaikh's female elephant was with him, and pointed out his wounded lord. As soon as Nar Singh saw him, he dismounted, and taking his head upon his knees, began to wipe his mouth with his own garment. Jabbar, observing from behind the tree that Nar Singh was in a compassionate mood, came forward and saluted him. Nar Singh asked who he was. Just then the Shaikh unclosed his eyes. Nar Singh, sitting as he was, saluted him, and telling his attendants to bring the *farmans,* said to the Shaikh with blandishment, "The all-conquering lord has sent for your courteously." The Shaikh looked bitterly at him. Nar Singh swore that he would carry him in safety to him. The Shaikh began to abuse him angrily. Nar Singh's attendants then told him he would not be able to convey him away, for the wound was mortal; upon hearing which, Jabbar drew his sword, and, slaying several Rajputs, had nearly reached Nar Singh, when they killed and trampled him under foot. Nar Singh then rose from the Shaikh's head, and his attendants despatched him, and cutting off the head of that great one, started off, meddling with no one else, but even releasing those whom they had taken prisoners.

OF MY DEPUTATION TO THE ARMY OF RAY-RAYAN TO INQUIRE INTO THE CONDUCT OF THE OFFICERS

After two or three months, news came from the army which had been sent under Ray-rayan to chastise Nar Singh. A number of the most distinguished officers had accompanied him, and Ziau-l Mulk Kasi was second in command. All at once despatches came from them to this effect: "We had completely routed Nar Singh, and driven him into the walled fort of Iraj, with a body of 400 Rajputs; we had invested the fort and made our approaches, and it seemed inevitable that he must fall into our hands the next day. The fort is situated on the banks of a broad deep river, the other three sides being exposed to the land. The general, Ray-rayan, undertook himself to guard the river bank, placing the other officers on the three remaining sides. At midnight, when sleep was heavy upon all, the Rajputs got out. Cutting through the wall on the river-side, they led their horses down the glacis, and mounting upon the river bank, crossed over at a place where there was some kind of a ford, passing through the Ray-rayan's elephant stable, and by the time your slaves and the other chiefs had discovered what had happened, he had advanced far on his way. By this stratagem he has escaped."

When the despatches had been read, the Emperor, who thirsted for the blood of that wretch, fell into the greatest conceivable passion, and turning to Shaikh Farid, said he must go and investigate by whose fault this had happened; for the Ray-rayan reports that Nar Singh escaped through the lines of the Raja of Gwalior, and the Raja, in his turn, writes that he passed through the camp of the general, while the second in command declares that treachery has been at work, as he was completely entrapped. In short, each lays the blame on the other. The Shaikh represented that Shaikh Abu-l Khair, 'Allami's brother, was very clever in investigations. As soon as he heard that name, His Majesty exclaimed, "I have it; send for Asad." It chanced that I was on guard that night, and sitting in the guard-room with Aka Mulla.

About eight o' clock messengers arrived with orders for me to come immediately to the fort. As soon as I was announced, His Majesty called for me. I made my obeisance, and seeing marks of anger and rage in the royal countenance, I feared he was about to put me to death. When His Majesty and the courtiers saw my alarm, they smiled, and throwing me the despatches, bade me read them. I first perused that of the Ray-rayan, and was proceeding with the rest, when he asked me whether I had understood the contents. I replied that I had partly done so. He said, "Now this has happened, do you go to the camp and inquire whose fault it is, and investigate the whole affair, for I am very much annoyed at this accident, and therefore have determined to send you." I made my obeisance, and replied that I would use my utmost endeavours to fail in nothing. . .

As soon as the Raja and all the officers were assembled, I produced a sheet made of pieces of cloth sown together, upon which was drawn a plan of the fort of Iraj, with the river on one side, and the gates and towers on the other three. The encampment of each chief was marked thereon, with the number of his forces. I then called Ziau-l Mulk, and made him write the name of each chief in the place which his forces had occupied, and made them all attach their seals to it. I also marked the place where Nar Sing had made his exit, and the spot at which he passed the river. When the chiefs had all affixed their seals to this sheet, I asked them whether they had thus represented it. After we had eaten betel and received perfumes, I took leave of all. The son of Muhammad Khan Tatar, a near connexion and relative of mine, was appointed to escort me with 1000 horse to

Gwalior. . . . I went myself with Musahib to the Court, and reported myself to Ram Das, who conducted me to the foremost railing, where I made my obeisance. His Majesty called me with the greatest impatience; and after presenting a gold *mohur* and nine rupees, I prostrated myself. His Majesty immediately said, "Whose fault was it?" I bowed, and replied that I would relate all particulars; but he again insisted that I should tell him what fault I thought there had been. Seeing his impatience, I replied, "I cannot say that any one has erred intentionally. There has only been great neglect, and all are alike guilty; that is my humble opinion." Shaikh Farid said, "Neglect is also a fault." I answered, "That is a fault which is committed intentionally, and that is carelessness which happens without any ill intention." I was going to say more to the Shaikh, when His Majesty rose, and said "Asad is right." From the way he spoke it was evident that he was very much pleased, and I saw that my words had been agreeable to him. . . .

OF MY APPOINTMENT TO BRING BACK MIR JAMALU-D DIN FROM THE DAKHIN

When the Emperor was at Burhanpur, he had sent Saiyid Mir Jamalu-d din Husain Inju on a misssion to 'Adil Khan Sawai, in order to form an alliance with him; for since that Prince had professed himself a follower of the Emperor, it was thought right to exalt him to the highest rank, by uniting his daughter in marriage with the high and fortunate Prince Daniyal. The Saiyid had gone about that business long before, and made such unnecessary delay, that the Emperor was displeased with him. Just at the time I am speaking of, a joint report from the Khan-i-khanan and the Saiyid reached the Emperor, written in such an improper spirit, to make excuses for further delay, that His Majesty became exceedingly angry, and exclaimed, "He has seduced that noble too from his allegiance. By God's will, I will send some one to bring him back with dishonour." He then cast a glance along the ranks of his servants, and when the lightning eyes of that shadow of God fell upon me, the least of his slaves, he called me, and caring as he did for the least, said to his great officers, "I will send Asad to bring him back without giving him time to eat or drink." Then turning to me he said, "I have appointed you to the Dakhin, on a service that will secure you abundant wealth."

. . . In a few days I had made all ready, and the royal *farmans* were all prepared. A very gracious *farman* was written with all possible courtesy to 'Adil Khan of Bijapur. Its contents were as follows: "We find by the despatches of the Saiyid that you desire the town of Gwalior.[4] Very good. If you are really anxious about the matter, open your mind to the faithful servant Asad, and we will issue orders according to your wish, and bestow it upon you for ever, so that you may appoint your own governor there." To Mir Jamalu-d din I bore orders to this effect: "If thou dost not return to Court with Asad, thou shalt see what will happen to thee and to thy children."

DESCRIPTION OF BIJAPUR

That palace, which they called Hajjah, was so arranged, that each house in it had a double court. Where there are two courts, they call it in those parts Hajjah. All round the gate of my residence were lofty buildings with houses and porticos; the situation was very healthy and airy. It lies in an open space in the city. Its northern portico is to the east of a *bazar* of great extent, as much as thirty yards wide and about two *kos* long. Before each shop was a beautiful green tree, and the whole *bazar* was extremely clean and pure. It was filled with rare goods, such as are not seen or heard of in any other

[4]*I have not been able to identify this Gwalior.—Ed.*

town. There were shops of cloth-sellers, jewellers, armourers, vintners, bakers, fishmongers, and cooks. To give some idea of the whole *bazar,* I will describe a small section in detail.

In the jewellers' shops were jewels of all sorts, wrought into a variety of articles, such as daggers, knives, mirrors, necklaces, and also into the form of birds, such as parrots, doves and peacocks, etc., all studded with valuable jewels, and arranged upon shelves, rising one above the other. By the side of this shop will be a baker's, with rare viands, placed in the same manner, upon tiers of shelves. Further on a linendraper's, with all kinds of cloths, shelved in like manner. Then a clothier's. Then a spirit-merchant's, with various sorts of china vessels, valuable crystal bottles, and costly cups, filled with choice and rare essences, arrayed on shelves, while in front of the shop were jars of double-distilled spirits. Beside that shop will be a fruiterer's, filled with all kinds of fruit and sweetmeats, such as pistachio-nuts, and relishes, and sugar-candy, and almonds.

On another side may be a wine-merchant's shop, and an establishment of singers and dancers, beautiful women adorned with various kinds of jewels, and fair-faced choristers, all ready to perform whatever may be desired of them. In short, the whole *bazar* was filled with wine and beauty, dancers, perfumes, jewels of all sorts, palaces, and viands. In one street were a thousand bands of people drinking, and dancers, lovers, and pleasure-seekers assembled; none quarrelled or disputed with another, and this state of things was perpetual. Perhaps no place in the wide world could present a more wonderful spectacle to the eye of the traveller.

AKBAR ORDERS A SERVANT TO BE THROWN OFF A TOWER

At that time the Emperor used to retire for a long interval, after evening prayers, during which time the servants and courtiers used to disperse, assembling again when they expected His Majesty to re-appear. That evening he happened to come out sooner than usual, to hear the news from the Dakhin, and at first found none of the servants in the palace. When he came near the throne and couch, he saw a luckless lamplighter, coiled up like a snake, in a careless death-like sleep, close to the royal couch. Enraged at the sight, he ordered him to be thrown from the tower, and he was dashed into a thousand pieces. In the midst of his anger, the unhappy Khwaja Amiru-d din, whose watch it was, came in sight. Akbar addressed him with harshness and anger, and after abusing and disgracing him, turned him out of the tower, and ordered him instantly to start off and join the Prince's camp. He severely reprehended Daulat Khan, who was also on guard at the time, and disgraced and dishonoured him. Even Ram Das had a share in that misfortune, but he was not so severely punished. The Emperor then sat down on the royal couch, and in great fear I approached and saluted him.

As soon as his eyes fell upon me, he bestowed upon me the office which Khwaja Amiru-d din had held for some years, and in which he had enjoyed great respect and honour, and at the same time said to Ram Das, "I have bestowed the office of that wretch on Asad: we shall see how he conducts himself. Bring him now to do homage."

INTRODUCTION OF TOBACCO

In Bijapur I had found some tobacco. Never having seen the like in India, I brought some with me, and prepared a handsome pipe of jewel work. The stem, the finest to be procured at Achin, was three cubits in length, beautifully dried and coloured, both ends being adorned with jewels and enamel. I happened to come across a very handsome mouthpiece of Yaman cornelian, oval-shaped, which I set to the stem; the whole was very handsome. There was also a golden burner for lighting it, as a proper accompaniment. 'Adil Khan had given me a betel bag, of very superior workmanship; this I filled with fine tobacco, such, that it one leaf be lit, the whole will continue burning. I arranged all elegantly on a silver tray. I had a silver tube made to keep the stem in, and that too was covered with purple velvet.

His Majesty was enjoying himself, after receiving my presents, and asking me how I had collected so many strange things in so short a time, when his eye fell upon the tray with the pipe and its appurtenances; he expressed great surprise, and examined the tobacco, which was made up in pipefuls; he inquired what it was, and where I had got it. The Nawab Khan-i 'Azam replied: "This is tobacco, which is well known in Mecca and Medina, and this doctor has brought it as a medicine for your Majesty." His Majesty looked at it, and ordered me to prepare and take him a pipeful. He began to smoke it when his physician approached and forbade his doing so. But His Majesty was graciously pleased to say he must smoke a little to gratify me, and taking the mouthpiece into his sacred mouth, drew two or three breaths. The physician was in great trouble and would not let him do more. He took the pipe from his mouth, and bid the Khan-i 'Azam try it, who took two or three puffs. He then sent for his druggist, and asked what were its peculiar qualities. He replied that there was no mention of it in his books; but that it was a new invention, and the stems were imported from China, and the European doctors had written much in its praise. The first physician said, "In fact, this is an untried medicine, about which the doctors have written nothing. How can we describe to Your Majesty the qualities of such unknown things? It is not fitting that Your Majesty should try it." I said to the first physician, "The Europeans are not so foolish as not to know all about it; there are wise men among them who seldom err or commit mistakes. How can you, before you have tried a thing and found out all its qualities, pass a judgment on it that can be depended on by the physicians, kings, great men and nobles? Things must be judged of according to their good or bad qualities, and the decision must be according to the facts of the case." The physician replied, "We do not want to follow the Europeans, and adopt a custom, which is not sanctioned by our own wise men, without trial." I said, "It is a strange thing, for every custom in the world has been new at one time or other; from the days of Adam till now, they have gradually been invented. When a new thing is introduced among a people, and becomes well known in the world, every one adopts it; wise men and physicians should determine according to the good or bad qualities of a thing; the good qualities may not appear at once. Thus the China root, not known anciently, has been newly discovered, and is useful in many diseases," When the Emperor heard me dispute and reason with the physician, he was astonished, and being much pleased, gave me his blessing, and then said to Khan-i 'Azam, "Did you hear now wisely Asad spoke? Truly, we must not reject a thing that has been adopted by the wise men of other nations merely because we cannot find it in our books; or how shall we progress?" The physician was going to say more, when His Majesty stopped him and called for the priest. The priest ascribed many good qualities to it, but no one could persuade the physician; nevertheless, he was a good physician.

As I had brought a large supply of tobacco and pipes, I sent some to several of the nobles, while others sent to ask for some; indeed, all, without exception, wanted some, and the practice was introduced. After that the merchants began to sell it, so the custom of smoking spread rapidly. His Majesty, however, did not adopt it.

MISSION TO THE DAKHIN

At last orders were passed, that royal *farmans* should be addressed to the governors of the provinces of the Dakhin, namely Bijapur, Golconda, Bidar, and the Carnatic. His Majesty said to me, "You went before, in great discomfort, to fetch, Mir Jamalu-d din and the daughter of 'Adil Khan and the presents, because it was necessary. But this time you must go in state to the four provinces of the Dakhin, and remain in each place so long as may be necessary, to collect whatever they may have of fine elephants and rare jewels throughout their dominions, to bring back with you. Their money you may keep. I want nothing but their choice and rare elephants and jewels. You must secure things of this kind for the Government, the rest I give you. You must not relax your efforts as long as there is one fine elephant or rare jewel out of your grasp in the Dakhin." In short, I was sent for these purposes. But nearly two months passed from the time of my first appointment before I received my dismissal. Again His Majesty said, "Don't trouble yourself about money; all those countries are at your disposal, and shall come to you." I made my preparations according to these gracious and kind orders. Though I was only a commander of 200, I enlisted 600 chosen horsemen of I'rak, Khurasan, and Turkistan; many among them being men of rank. To each servant I gave a fine horse and three or four months' pay in advance. Even commanders of 1000 or 2000 could not boast of so well-accoutred a train as was then assembled. I appointed Shah 'Ali of Ispahan, a beautiful writer, as my *bakhshi,* and hired 100 musketeers, 100 guards and servants, and 100 archers. In short, I made great preparations.

ACCOUNT OF THE DEATH OF HIS MAJESTY, AND OF OTHER MATTERS IN CONNEXION WITH IT

As I, Asad, wandering in the wood of evil destiny, had

started for the second time as envoy to the four southern provinces, Bijapur, Golconda, Bidar, and the Carnatic, I was not present when that peerless sovereign departed this life. When the question of my embassy was in agitation, the Emperor was also projecting a combat between the elephants Chanchal and Giranbar. His Majesty, now at rest, ordered me not to depart till I had seen the elephant fight; but Fate had ordained otherwise, and I was not sorry for it, for, as I shall relate, His Majesty had cause for severe anger at that elephant fight, which came off after my departure.

A few days after I left Agra, His Majesty had been taken somewhat ill, and in a short time was very much broken down. While he was in this condition, the combat of the elephant Chanchal with the elephant Giranbar, belonging to the royal Prince, came off. While the fight was going on, an angry dispute arose between the servants of Prince Salim, and Sultan Khusru, and both overstepped the bounds of courtesy. When His Majesty heard of it, he became exceedingly angry, vexed, and enraged, and this so much increased his illness, that the chief physician, one of the most skilful of his time in the healing art, could do nothing more. During the Emperor's illness the weight of affairs fell upon the Khan-i 'Azam, and when it became evident that the life of that illustrious sovereign was drawing to a close, he consulted with Raja Man Singh, one of the principal nobles, and they agreed to make Sultan Khusru Emperor. They were both versed in business and possessed of great power, and determined to seize the Prince (Salim), when he came, according to his daily custom, to pay his respects at Court, thus displaying the nature of their mind, little considering that the sun cannot be smeared with mud, nor the marks of the pen of destiny be erased by the pen-knife of treachery. He whom the hand of the power of Allah upholds, though he be helpless in himself, is safe from all evil.

The next day that chosen one of Allah, not dreaming of the treachery of his foes, went, as was his wont, to pay his respects at Court, and entered a boat with several of his attendants. They had reached the foot of the tower, and were about to disembark, when Mir Ziau-l Mulk of Kazwin arrived in great agitation, and jumped into the boat. He brought word of the hopeless state of the Emperor, and of the treachery and perfidy of those evil men. The boat returned, and His Royal Highness, with weeping eyes and a sore heart, re-entered his private palace. So that, through the endeavours of that faithful friend and sincere well-wisher, the arrow of those perfidious enemies missed its mark.

When the raw attempt of those wretches had thus been brought to light, and the lofty-flying phoenix had escaped their treacherous snare, and the curtain which concealed their intentions had been torn, they were obliged to throw off all dissimulation.

At that time the breath was still in the Emperor's body, and all his servants and officers were assembled in the audience-room in great distress and agitation. The Khan-i 'Azam and Raja Man Singh sat down, and calling all the nobles together, began to consult with them, and went so far as to say, "The character of the high and mighty Prince Sultan Salim is well known, and the Emperor's feelings towards him are notorious; for he by no means wishes him to be his successor. We must all agree to place Sultan Khusru upon the throne." When this was said, Saiyid Khan, who was one of the great nobles, and connected with the royal house, and descended from an ancient and illustrious Mughal family, cried out, "Of what do you speak, that in the existence of a Prince like Salim Shah, we should place his son upon the throne! This is contrary to the laws and customs of the Chaghatai Tatars, and shall never be." He and Malik Khair, who was also a great chief and well skilled in business, with others, of their opinion, rose and left the assembly.

The Khan-i 'Azam, who was at the bottom of all these evil designs, concealed his rage, and could say nothing. The assembly broke up, and each went his own way. Raja Ram Das Kachhwaha, with all his followers, immediately went to guard the treasury, and Murtaza Khan left the fort, and retiring to his own residence, took steps to assemble the Saiyids of Barah and his own followers. Meanwhile Mirza Sharif and Mu'tamad Khan came and asked him what he intended to do. Knowing them to be his friends, he said, "I intend to go to the Prince." Mu'tamad Khan expressed his readiness to do the same, and Murtaza Khan bade him go first to the Prince, and say that he would be there immediately with his followers. So he went to His Royal Highness.

As soon as the Prince, following the advice of Mir Zia, had retired to his own palace, all the foolish people round him began to alarm him, saying, "Why does Your Highness sit careless here? Your enemies have completed their work, and placed Sultan Khusru on the throne, and declare that they will point the guns of the fort against this house." Their evil counsels were nearly taking effect upon the Prince, and he was about to order his private boats, to save himself by flight, when Shaikh Ruknu-d din Rohilla, one of his best servants, who had a large body of followers, and was a man of known courage, came and besought him to compose himself, and wait for two hours to see what would happen. The Prince was still occupied in listening to this brave advice, when all at once Mirza Sharif came in, and told him how the assembly of his enemies had broken up, and that Murtaza Khan was coming to join him. His Royal Highness was much delighted and began to encourage his people, when Fara Beg came and made salutations, and Mir Murtaza Khan arrived with a large body of attendants and may of the noble Saiyids of Barah, and saluting him, began to beat the drums to celebrate the day. The Prince forbad the music, on account of the sad state of the Emperor, but honoured Mir Murtaza Khan with a special dress of honour and a jewelled scimitar. People began to flock in, each striving to be the first to arrive, till at last, in the evening, the Khan-i 'Azam came in great shame and paid his respects. The Prince took not the least notice of his ill-conduct, and bestowed all royal kindness upon him.

When Raja Man Singh saw the change in the aspect of affairs, he took Sultan Khusru with him to his own palace, and prepared boats, intending to escape the next day to Bengal. As soon as the Prince was relieved from all anxiety as to the course affairs were taking, he went with the great nobles, and Mir Murtaza Khan at their head, without fear, to the fort, and approached the dying Emperor. He was still breathing, as if he had only waited to see that illustrious one. As soon as that most fortunate Prince entered, he bowed himself at the feet of His Majesty. He saw that he was in his last agonies. The Emperor once more opened his eyes, and signed to them to invest him with the turban and robes which had been prepared for him, and to gird him with his own dagger. The attendants prostrated themselves and did homage; at the same moment that sovereign, whose sins are forgiven, bowed himself also and closed his life. A loud lamentation rose on all sides, and groans and cries ascended from the world and race of men, and the voices of the angelic cherubims were heard saying, "God created him, and to God he has returned."

When the Emperor Akbar died,
Groans arose from Earth to Heaven.

After that sad occurrence, that gracious Emperor Jahangir bade all his confidential servants and faithful friends perform the obsequies of the deceased sovereign, with all the ceremonies due to his rank. When they had gone through the funeral rites prescribed by religion and tradition, and had arrayed the royal corpse in all state, the Emperor, in great pomp, with weeping eyes and a sad heart, took the foot of the bier of the deceased King upon his shoulder, and carried it as far as the door of the public reception room; from thence, the great nobles, each anxious for the honour, relieving one another in quick succession, carried His Majesty as far as the gate of the fort. Thence the nobles and ministers, and courtiers and *imams,* and all his servants and troops, followed the bier with heads and feet uncovered . . . .

When His Majesty had concluded this necessary business, he entrusted the fort and treasury to Raja Ram Das, and praised and consoled him much. Leaving the fort, he then went to his own palace. where intelligence reached him that Raja Man Singh, taking with him Sultan Khusru, was embarking on board boats for Bengal, with all his servants and troops. Although the royal heart was vexed at hearing this, yet he sent Madhav Singh, his brother, who was present, to re-assure and bring him back. Madhav Singh went to the Raja, and reproving him strongly, asked what he meant by acting thus towards such a sovereign, and of what use it was? He replied, "What can I do? The Prince is young, and knew nothing of all these matters. I was obliged to act as I have done, to satisfy him." Do you go and say, 'Let a promise be given that he may be relieved from all fear, and that I may be satisfied that no harm will befall him, and I will bring him to your Majesty's feat." Madhav Singh returned and reported Raja Man Singh's wishes and petition to His Majesty, who gave his promise, with the utmost grace and kindness, that no harm should happen to him from any one, and sent him back confirming his word with solemn oaths. The next day Raja Man Singh came to Court, and brought Sultan Khusru to the feet of his royal father. His Majesty treated him with the greatest kindness, and clasping him to his bosom. kissed his face. After a moment he dismissed him to his own house. When His Majesty had concluded that business, he passed some days in mourning and distributing alms, till at last the day arrived for him to ascend the throne.

Of the ascension of His Majesty the Emperor Nuru-d din Muhammad Jahangir to the throne of his fathers and ancestors

On that day he held a Court, and after going through all the usual ordinances, left his own palace in great pomp and state, with all show and grandeur, and embarking in a boat, went to the fort, where he disembarked, and mounting the stately litter, entered the fort scattering gold and silver. There all the nobles of rank and powerful ministers were in attendance. When he arrived, he ascended the throne of the Empire, and after adopting the title of Jahangir, began to win the hearts of all the people, and to re-arrange the withered world. He honoured many of the greatest nobles and powerful ministers and brave youths with honourable titles and acceptable dignities; for the consolation of the hearts of his people, he suspended the chain of justice with golden bells, and removed the rust of oppression from the hearts of his people . . . .

Some days after his ascension, intelligence arrived that Muhabat Khan and Sharif Khan, who were of the highest rank in the Empire, had come to offer their congratulations. Muhabat Khan was made commander-in-chief, and Sharif Khan was honoured with the title of Amiru-l 'Umara. Day by day the Empire of that just and liberal sovereign increased in splendour and efficiency. In the first few days he repealed and gave up all transit duties, and fees, the poll-tax on Hindus and tax on orphans' property, and remitted them throughout the whole of the hereditary dominions. He also remitted and removed, root and branch, the whole of the duties and imposts levied on the produce of the sea or of mines, so that throughout the whole of Hindustan, and wherever the jurisdiction of the Emperor extended, no one could so much as name them.

TARIKH-I HAKKI[5]

OF

SHAIKH 'ABDU-L HAKK

THIS work contains a brief general history of Muhammadan India, from the time of the slave-kings of Dehli to that of Akbar, in the forty-second year of whose reign it was composed, i.e., A.H. 1005 (A. D. 1596-7). The name of the author is Shaikh 'Abdu-l Hakk bin Saifu-d din of Dehli. From a quartrain in the preface of his history, it would appear that Hakki, "the true," while it contains a play upon his own name, is a mere literary appellation, assumed according to a practice common in the east, and by which name he seems to wish that his history should be known, though it is most frequently styled *Tarikh-i 'Abdu-l Hakk*

The ancestors of 'Abdu-l Hakk came into India from Bokhara, and settled in Dehli, but the authorities vary in the details they give in respect of him. According to the *Badshah-nama,* 'Abdu-l Hakk was a descendant of one of Timur's followers, who remained behind, together with some other foreign chiefs, at Dehli, after the return of that conqueror to his native land. But the writer himself, in his *Akhbaru-l Akhyar,* says that his great ancestor, Agha Turk, came to Dehli in 'Alau-d din's reign, and that this Agha's grandson, Malik Musa, returned to Mawarau-n nahr, and came back from thence to Dehli in Timur's time. In Sir T. Metcalfe's MS. History of Delhi it is stated that his ancestor was a native of Bokhara, who, on visiting Dehli, was ennobled and

[5]*See Asaru-s Sanadid, p.* 80, *Tabakat-i Shah-jahani; Mirat-i Jahan-numa; Ma-asiru-l Kiran, p.* 256, *Zubdatu-l Gharaib* (*extract, post*); *Beale,* 364.

attached to the Royal Court. There can be no doubt that Bokhara was the place from which they sprang, as 'Abdu-l Hakk's son was known as "al Dehlawi al Bokhari." 'Abdu-l Hakk's father obtained a reputation for sanctity, and the son praises him in his Literary History of Dehli.

Shaikh 'Abdu-l Hakk early applied himself to the cultivation of knowledge. At twenty years of age he had mastered most of the customary branches of education, and had learnt the whole of the *Kuran* by heart.[6] At the time he was prosecuting his studies, the author[7] tells us that he used to go twice a day to college, morning and evening, during the heat of one season and the cold of another, returning for a short time for a meal to his own house. As he informs us that his dwelling was two miles from the college, this statement, if true, shows that he travelled eight miles a day, which, it must be confessed, exhibited unusual ardour in the acquisition of knowledge. His father observed that he did not enjoy pastimes like other boys, and endeavoured to dissuade him from his intense application.

Upon leaving Dehli, he associated for a long time with 'Abdu-l Kadir, Shaikh Faizi, and Nizamu-d din, at Fathpur,[8] but left them upon some slight misunderstanding. Nevertheless, through the interest of the latter, he obtained a passage on a vessel proceeding to Arabia, whither he went on a pilgrimate.[9] He dwelt for a long time in the holy cities of Mecca and Medina, and derived much instruction from the learned men of those cities. He wrote works upon many subjects, of which he himself

[6] *Badshah-nama of 'Abdu-l Hamid Lahori (MS. fol.* 451 *v.).*

[7] *Akhbaru-l Akhyar (MS. fol.* 354 *v.).*

[8] *Tarikh-i Badauni of 'Abdu-l Kadir (MS. fol* 228 *r.)*

[9] *Sir T. Metcalfe's Memoir of Dehli says that he made the pilgrimage twice.*

gives a list,—commentaries, travels, *Sufi* doctrines, religion and history, and his different treatises amount altogether to more than one hundred. The best known are the *Madina Sakina,* the *Madariju-n Nubuwat,* the *Jazbu-l Kulub,*[10] and the *Akhbaru-l Akhyar.* He was born in the year 958 H., and in the year 1047 H., although he was then ninety years old, he is said[11] to have been in full possession of his faculties, and to have employed himself in religious duties, in instruction, and composition, as vigorously as if he had still been a young man. He died in 1052 H., (1642 A.D.), and was buried in the sepulchre built by himself in Dehli on the margin of the Hauz-i Shamshi. The building still exists in good preservation, and is a handsome solid structure.

The author, who now holds a high rank among the saints of Hindustan, informs us that his desire to write history arose from a perusal of the *Tarikh-i Firoz-shahi,* by which he alludes to that of Ziau-d din Barni, as he mentions that the lives of several kings are contained in it, which is not the case with the other histories of that name. But as the work concludes with the beginning of Firoz Shah's reign, he sought to obtain information respecting the kings who succeeded him, and lighted upon the *Tarikh-i Bahadur-Shahi,* written by Sam Sultan Bahadur Gujrati, from which he has extracted down to the reign of Bahlol Lodi. He then thought it would be advisable to complete the reigns previous to those noticed in the *Tarikh-i Firoz-shahi,* and therefore abstracted from the *Tabakat-i Nasiri* the reigns from *Mu'izzu-d din Sam* (Muhammad Ghori) to Nasiru-d din Mahmud bin Sultan Shamsu-d din. He has been judicious in his small selec-

[10]*This is a history of Medina, which was commenced in that city in A.H.* 998, *and has been very well printed in Calcutta.*

[11]*Badshah-nama.*

tion, as these three are the best authorities for their respestive periods.[12] From Bahlol Lodi to his own time he has depended on verbal information, and upon what came under his own observation, all the rest of his work being taken, as he candidly confesses, verbatim from the three authors above quoted.

After carrying, in the first chapter, the general history of Dehli down to Akbar's time, he gives, in the second, a compendious account of the rulers of Bengal, Jaunpur, Mandu, Dakhin, Multan, Sind and Kashmir, but the narrative is much too brief to be of any use.

As this time-serving saint was prepared to speak of his reforming patron in the preposterous strain of adulation adopted in the following Extract, we have little reason to regret that he never fulfilled the purpose of writing an account of his reign.

The best copy of this little history which I have seen belongs to Nawab Nasiru-d din Ahmad of Panipat, in whose collection it is improperly called *Tarikh-i Salatin Ghori*. Nizamu-d din, a physician resident at Banda, also possesses a good copy. There are two copies (Addit. MSS. 6596 and 16701) in the British Museum, and one in the Library of the Royal Asiatic Society, which Morley has described in his Catalogue (No. xlvii).

In a Manuscript belonging to an Indian gentleman at Dehli, the first chapter closes with these words, "Thus ends the first chapter of the *Tazkiratu-s Salatin*," which would imply that this work is known by that name; but, if so, it cannot be the work generally,[13] known as the *Tazkiratu-s Salatin*, for that is devoted to an account of the Hindu dynasties, and upon that compliation Colonel Wildford, in his essay on Vikramaditya and Salivahana, makes the following just observations: "This treatise is

[12] *Briggs, vol. iv. pp.* 131-392.
[13] *See Reinaud's Memoire, p.* 6.

a most perfect specimen of the manner of writing history in India; for, excepting the above list, almost everything else is the production of the fertile genius of the compiler. In all these lists the compilers and revisers seem to have had no other object in view, but to adjust a certain number of remarkable epochs. This being once effected, the intermediate spaces are filled up with names of kings not to be found anywhere else, and most probably fanciful. Otherwise they leave out the names of those kings of whom nothing is recorded, and attribute the years of their reign to some among them better known, and of greater fame. They often do not scruple to transpose some of those kings, and even whole dynasties; either in consequence of some preconceived opinion, or owing to their mistaking a famous king for another of the same name. It was not uncommon with ancient writers, to pass from a remote ancestor to a remote descendant; or from a remote predecessor to a remote successor, by leaving out the intermediate generations or successions, and sometimes ascribing the years of their reigns, to a remote successor or predecessor. In this manner the lists of the ancient kings of Persia, both by Oriental writers, and others in the west, have been compiled: and some instances of this nature might be produced from Scripture. I was acquainted lately, at Benares, with a chronicler of that sort, and in the several conversations I had with him, he candidly acknowledged that he filled up the intermediate spaces between the reigns of famous kings with names at a venture; that he shortened or lengthened their reigns at pleasure; and that it was understood that his predecessors had taken the same liberties. Through their emendations and corrections, you see plainly a total want of historical knowledge and criticism; and sometimes some disingenuity is but too obvious. This is, however, the case with the sections on futurity in the Bhagvat, Vayu, Vishnu, and Brahmanda Puranas; which with the above lists constitute the whole stock of historical knowledge among the Hindus; and the whole might be comprised in a few quarto pages of print."[14]

The *Tarikh-i Hakki* opens with a passage from the Kuran.

The conclusion varies. The most perfect closes with a chronogram, which would seem to show that the author wished his work to be styled *Zikr-i Muluk,* and from another passage this appears to be the true name, though the preface, as before observed, authorizes the name of *Tarikh-i Hakki.*

The copy used is a small 8 vo., containing 142 pages, of 18 lines each.

EXTRACT

Shortly after ascending the throne, Firoz Shah was murdered by his maternal uncle Mubariz Khan. Salim Shah had anticipated this, and had therefore asked his wife's consent to kill her brother Mubariz, saying that if she did not accede to his proposal, she would not long see her son alive. The senseless woman did not believe his words, and would not give her consent; but it turned out as Salim Shah had predicted. Firoz Shah reigned not more than three days and five hours. After his murder, all his Afghan relations claimed the throne. One assumed the title of Sikandar, another of Sultan Ibrahim, and a third of Sultan Muhammad 'Adil. The rivals contested the point amongst themselves most pertinaciously for three or four years, when, at length, in the month of Shawwal, in the year 963, the Huma of Humayun again spread the wings of its prosperity and good luck over the kingdom of Hindustan. The dust of distress which had long obscured the beautiful face of the kingdom was washed away by the water of peace and union, and the heart of the country was invigorated by a new infusion of life. Joy and gladness, gratitude and boundless hope,

[14] *Asiatic Researches, vol. ix. pp.* 132, 133.

were diffused among all people, both high and low, rich and poor.

Within six months of the second reign Humayun, while standing one evening enjoying the fresh air on the top of the red palace in the fort of Dehli, heard the *azan* called, and sitting down out of respect to the summons to evening prayer, his foot slipped by accident, and he fell to the ground. He died on the spot, or at least a few days afterwards, and the bird of his victorious soul fled to its nest in Paradise. From God we proceed, to God shall we return!

He was succeeded by his Son Sultan Abu-l Fath Jalalu-d din Muhammad Akbar Badshah Ghazi, of super-eminent dignity, etc. He ascended the throne in his youth, and though more than forty years have elapsed since his reign began, he is still in the very bloom of his dominion, and in the commencement of his power, for every day brings accounts of new victories and new conquests, so that by the blessing of God his kingdom extends over the whole of Hindustan (which is called "Chahar-dang," that is, a quarter of the world), east and west, north and south, including all its forts and teritories, without any one being associated with him in power, and without any one daring to offer opposition. This country is bounded on three sides by the sea, and all the kings and princes, chiefs, nobles, and Rajas, and all people, of every degree, throughout the whole country, pay allegiance to him, willingly acknowledge him as their sovereign, and place the head of abject submission on the ground in his presence. Territories, treasures, elephants, horses, armies, and all other things, suitable to the state and dignity of Emperors, came into his possession in such abundance, that they are beyond all calculation, and are of a value far exceeding anything which has ever yet been in the possession of other Emperors.

"This monarch, at the very commencement of his reign, effected that which kings who have reigned many years have not been able to accomplish.'' "God can place the whole world in the hands of one person!"

The kings and Sultans, who have been spoken of in this book, are not worthy of those titles in the presence of the exalted Majesty of Akbar, with the exception, perhaps, of one or two individuals; but to call even them kings, in comparison, requires no small degree of courage and resolution.

In short, it is difficult to describe the victories and conquests of the Emperor Akbar, his rules and regulations, his principles of government, his extraordinary orders, his courteous manners, and the many innovations which he introduced. Entire volumes and registers would not contain them. If I be blessed with a long life, and if I receive the aid of God, I shall atempt to the utmost of my power to write, free from error, the history of the Emperor. May it be the will of God that, through the aid of this omnipotent Emperor of Emperors, the Muhammadan law and religion may be established for ever and ever. "O God of the worlds, accept this prayer!"

ZUBDATU-T TAWARIKH[1]

OF

SHAIKH NURU-L HAKK

THIS is a general history, composed by Shaikh Nuru-l Hakk, al-Mashriki, al-Dehlivi, al-Bokhari, the son of Abdu-l Hakk, noticed in the preceding article. The addition of al-Mashriki would imply that his family had changed their abode from Dehli to some district of Jaunpur.

Nuru-l Hakk's work is an enlarged edition of his father's history, and was composed, as the author informs us, in order that, by improving the style, and supplying omissions, he might render it worthy of the acceptance of his patron, Shaik Faridu-d din Bokhari, with whom he was connected by marriage, and who suggested the undertaking. It is for this reason that a large space is devoted to an account of Shaikh Faridu-d din's expeditions during the time of Akbar, and an interesting detail is given of his proceedings in Kashmir, the Khyber hills, Jammu, Jasrauta, Ramgarh, and other places in the Siwalik hills.[2] The same officer was subsequently appointed to the pursuit of Khusru in the early part of Jahangir's reign, in which expedition he acquired credit for considerable gallantry, and under the title of Murtaza Khan, managed for some time the affairs of the empire.

The work commences with the reign of Kutbu-d din, and ends with the close of Akbar's reign. (Much of the

[1]*See Mir-at-i Jahan-numa, p.* 660; *Tabakat-i Shahjahani, fol.* 310; *Ma-asiru-l Kiran, p.* 258; *Subhatu-l Marjan.*

[2]*No doubt copied from the "Akbar-nama" of Faizi Sirhindi.*

early part is copied verbatim or in abstract from the *Tabakat-i Nasiri,* the *Tarikh* of Zia Barni, the *Tarikh-i Mubarak Shahi,* and other works, as will be seen from the Extracts which follow). The reign of Akbar is copiously abstracted from the *Akbar-nama.* This is by far the most valuable part of the work, for besides what he copies from Abu-l Fazl, the author writes much from his own knowledge of contemporary events. A hope is held out that the author may be able to continue the work, and detail some of the events of Jahangir's reign, of whom he was contemporary. The author's father, 'Abdu-l Hakk, highly lauds the work in his *Literary History,* p. 43.

The Dakhin history is much more meagre than the rest. The history of the Bahmani, Nizam-shahi, 'Adil-shahi, Kutub-shahi dynasties is promised, but is not given. Berar, Bidr, Khandesh, are also omitted from this work, as they are from the *Tabakat-i Akbari,* which fact would of itself raise a suspicion that Nuru-l Hakk copied more than he acknowledged.

CONTENTS:—History of the kings of Dehli, from pp. 13 to 369. History of the kings of Malwa, from pp. 369 to 418. History of the kings of Gujarat, from pp. 418 to 458. History of the kings of the Dakhin, from pp. 458 to 482. History of the kings of Kashmir, from pp. 482 to 506. History of the kings of Sind and Thatta, from pp 507 to 514. History of the kings of Multan, from pp. 514 to 516. History of the kings of Bengal, from pp. 532 to 542. SIZE—Larfie 8 vo. comprising 542 pages, of 16 lines to a page.

By Muhammad Hashim, the author of the *Muntakhabu-l Lubab,* this history is styled the *Tarikh-i Zubda.* The name of *Zubdatu-t Tawarikh* is very common, and besides the history of this name, which will be noticed in another part of this work, there are two which have a classical reputation both in the east and west; one by Hafiz Abru, noticed elsewhere, the other by Jamalu-d din

Abu-l kasim Kashi. There is one also of a later date by Kamal Khan bin Jalal Munajjim. It is a general history, but chiefly devoted to Persia, the history of which it brings down to the close of the sixteenth century[3] Juwaini, in his *Jahan-Kusha,* notices another written by Saiyid Sadru-d din.

The *Zubdatu-t Tawarikh* of Nuru-l Hakk is not uncommon in India. One of the best manuscripts belongs to Nawab Siraju-l Mulk, Minister of Haidarabad, and 'Ali Muhammad Khan has a good copy. There is a copy in the British Museum, Addit. 10580, and one in the Bibliotheque Imperiale, No. 38, Supp. Persan. This professes to have been completed on Tuesday, 27 Rabiu-l awwal, 1067 H., so that it must be an early copy, unless this date be that of the composition.

EXTRACTS

(Several which appeared in Sir H. M. Elliot's original volume have been here omitted, as they have already been printed in the notices of the original works from which Nuru-l Hakk copied them).

Ṣultan Raziya

(Abstracted from the *Tabakat-i Nasiri*) *Sultans Mu'izzu-d din Kaikubad, 'Alau-d din and Kutbu-d din.* (Abstracted from the *Tarikh-i Firoz-shahi* of Zia Barni).

SULTAN MUHAMMAD, SON OF TUGHLIK SHAH

It was about this time that the whole of the Doab became unable any longer to bear up against the grievous rack-renting and oppressive taxes. The people in despair set fire to their barns and stacks, and carrying away their cattle, became wanderers in the wide world. Upon this, the Sultan gave orders that every such peasant who might be seized should be put to death, and that the whole coun-

[3] *See Morley's Catalogue, No. xliii.*

try should be ravaged and given up to indiscriminate plunder. He even himself marched out of the city for that purpose, as if he had been going on a hunting expedition, put to the sword all the remaining population, and ordered their heads to be displayed from the battlements of the fort. In this way he utterly depopulated whole tracts of his kingdom, and inflicted such rigorous punishment, that the whole world stood aghast. In short, the cruelties of this tyrant, whom some men call the Just, surpass all belief.

GHIYASU-D DIN TUGHLIK SHAH[4]

Upon the death of King Firoz, Tughlik Shah, the son of Prince Fath Khan, was raised to the throne in the palace of Firozabad. Having distributed among his nobles the high offices of the empire, he despatched a large army against Sultan Muhammad Shah, who, after a slight resistance, proceeded from Sirmur to Suket, whence he fled to Nagarkot, being pursued by the army of Tughlik Shah.

Under the influence of his youthful passions, Tughlik Shah gave himself up to debauchery and frivolity, and having but little experience in the concerns of government, thought it incumbent on him to imprison his own brother, Khuram Arslan Shah; upon which Abu Bakr, son of Zafar Khan, the son of Sultan Firoz, actuated by the fear and suspicion arising from the fate of the Prince, took to flight. Malik Ruknu-d din, the deputy *wazir*, and a number of other nobles, joined Abu Bakr, marched out and put Malik Mubarak Kabir to death, before the entrance of Tughlik Shah's palace at Firozabad, and the King, alarmed at the superior power of the rebels, fled with Khan Jahan through the gate facing the Jumna. Malik Ruknu-d din pursued and seized him, and putting him and his followers to death, suspended their heads from that gate. "What pleasures are there

[4]*From the Tarikh-i Mubarak-shahi.*

under the sky? The kid frolics before the butcher's shambles."

This event occurred on the 21st Safar, 791 A.H. Tughlik Shah reigned six months and eighteen days.

Abu Bakr, son of Zafar Khan, son of Sultan Firoz

Abu Bakr was placed on the throne with the title of Abu Bakr Shah. After subjugating his enemies, and possessing himself of the treasure and retinue of Firoz Shah, he became all-powerful.

Sultan Muhammad, proceeding from Nagarkot to Samana, proclaimed himself king, and commenced collecting an army. Hundreds of the nobles of Samana and the owners of lands situated at the foot of the hills, acknowledged his supreme authority. Some of the nobles, deserting Abu Bakr Shah, did Sultan Muhammad homage. The Sultan marched well equipped on Dehli from Samana, and by the time he reached the environs of that city, he had collected a body of cavalry to the amount of 50,000 men. On the 25th Rabi'u-l askhir, 791 A.H. he reached the palace of Jahan-numai.

On the 2nd of Jumada-l awwal a battle was fought between the Sultan Muhammad Jang and Abu Bakr Shah, in which the former sustained a total defeat. Crossing the Jumna with 2000 horse, he entered the Doab, and sent back his son, named Humayun Khan to Samana, with orders to collect an army and join him. He himself continued at Jalesar, near the banks of the Jumna.

A fresh army of 50,000 horse and foot was accordingly raised. In the month of Sha'ban of the same year, Sultan Muhammad marched on Dehli a second time, and again encountered Abu Bakr Shah. But Sultan Muhammad's fortune being still unpropitious, he was defeated in this battle likewise. "Though you make the dust of battle rise like columns of smokes, yet will your bravery be unavailing, if fortune does not favour you. If the key is not in your hand, no force will enable you to wrench open the door of victory."

Sultan Muhammad Shah, still continuing at Jalesar, issued orders to the people of Multan, Lahore, and several other places, directing them to kill the dependents of Firoz Shah, wherever they might find them. Accordingly a general massacre and great devastation ensued, roads were closed, travelling ceased, and houses were desolated.

In the month of Muharram, 792 A.H., Prince Humayun Khan marched out, accompanied by several of the nobles, and laid waste the environs of Dehli, but Abu Bakr Shah, despatching a force to oppose him, put him to flight.

SULTAN SIKANDAR SHAH LODI

About this time (900 A.H.) the scarcity of corn was so great that the people were relieved of the established *zakat*.

It is said that one day a Brahman declared in the presence of several Muhammadans that the religion of Islam was true, but that his own religion was also true. When this declaration reached the ear of the Doctors, they reported it to the Sultan and as he was remarkably fond of religious and legal questions and theological controversies, he summoned the learned from various quarters, and invited their opinion on what the Brahman had asserted. The learned gave it unanimously as their opinion that he should be imprisoned, and that he should then be desired to embrace Islam, and if he should reject it, that he should be slain. Accordingly, when the Brahman was desired to embrace the Muhammadan religion, he refused to do so, and he was put to death. Many other similar instances of his zeal for religion occurred during his reign . . .

In his time, Hindu temples were razed to the ground, and neither name nor vestige of them was allowed to remain. In the city of Mathura, if a Hindu wished to have his head or beard shaved, there was not a barber that dared to comply. He prohibited the procession of the spear of Salar Mas'ud Ghazi, which went every year to Bahraich, and women were not allowed to go on pilgrimages to shrines.

SULTAN IBRAHIM, SON OF SIKANDAR LODI

(*Same as the Tarikh-i Daudi*)

SHER KHAN

In the year 950 H. Puran-mal, son of Salhdi, held occupation of the fort of Raisin, and brought several of the neighbouring *parganas* under subjection. He had 1000 women in his *harem*, from the east and from Sind, and amongst them several Musulmanis, whom he made to dance before him. Sher Khan, with Musulman indignation, resolved to conquer the fort. After he had been some time engaged in investing it, an accommodation was proposed, and it was finally agreed that Puran-mal, with his family and children, and 4000 Rajputs of note, should be allowed to leave the fort ummolested. Several men learned in the law gave it as their opinion that they should all be slain, notwithstanding the solemn engagement which had been entered into. Consequently, the whole army, with the elephants, surrounded Puran-mal's encampment. The Rajputs fought with desperate bravery, and after killing their women and children and then burning them, they rushed to battle, and were annihilated to a man.

After that, Sher Khan retired to Agra, and after remaining there some time, set out on an expedition to Marwar, and at every stage he dug an entrenchment and raised a temporary fortress, advancing with the greatest care and circumspection. Whenever he met with a sandy soil and could not raise a fortress, he had sacks filled with sand, and heaping them up he constructed a defensible position out of them . . .

Sher Khan made the road which now runs from Dehli to Agra, by cutting through pungles, removing obstacles, and building *sarais.* Before that time, people had to travel through the Doab between those two places. There was so much security in travelling during his reign, that if a lone woman were to sleep in a desert with silver and gold about her person, no one would dare to commit theft upon her; and if it ever did so happen that any one lost any property, the *mukaddams* of the village which was the scene of the robbery were subject to fine, and for fear of its infliction, the *zamindars* used to patrol the roads at night.

Sher Khan founded many cities after his own name, as Sher-garh, Sher-kot; and since old Dehli was far from the river Jumna, he demolished it, and founded a new city on the banks of the river, which exists to this day. He founded also for its defence a broad wall, which, through the absence of rebellion and the length of his reign, was brought to completion.

It is said that once, when looking in a glass, he exclaimed, "Alas! that I have attained the empire only when I have reached old age, and when the time for evening prayer has arrived. Had it been otherwise, the world would have seen what I would have accomplished." Sometimes he would say, by way of showing what difficult and even impossible objects he contemplated; "I would have made a bridge to span the ocean, and have so contrived that even a widowed and helpless woman might without difficulty perform the pilgrimage to Mecca." To this day there exists a caravanserai of his building at Mecca in which Afghan *fakirs* reside.

THE REIGN OF AKBAR

Religious Matters

Up to this time (986 H., 1578 A.D.) the King used to attend public worship at the five stated times, whether he was in the capital or in camp, and the reciters of the

Kuran, who were on the royal establishment, used to read that sacred took both at prayer and at other times. Indeed, the King himself used to take the lead in worship.

One of the strange incidents of this year (986 H.) was the King's abandonment of the national religion, which became a stumbling-block to many people weak in the faith. The cause of this dereliction was, that the court had become the centre of attraction to all sects, persuasions, and people, to the learned of Khurasan, 'Irak, Mawarau-n nahr, and Hindustan, to doctors and theologians, to Shias and Sunnis, to Christians and philosophers, to Brahmans and professors of every existing religion. These all upon hearing not only of the King's affability, and condescension, but his superiority to all others in regal dignity and power, as well as in humility, flocked to his presence, and occupying themselves with relations of history and travels, and dissertations about revelations, prophecies, and religions, were perpetually engaged in angry controversies, and, as generally happens with confirmed disputants, all were eager to draw others to their own views and persuations, and passed day and night in "yeaing and naying." As this was the first time that the King had heard these discussions upon past history, customs, and religions of other nations, he was much struck with the novelty. He endeavoured to extract what was good from the contrary opinions which were expressed, giving the most deliberate attention to all that he heard, for his mind was solely bent upon ascertaining the truth. If some of his companions had their dispositions and sentiments affected by the inherent sin of their nature during these controversies, and became unable to withstand the temptations to apostacy, that is another matter; love of the world may have actuated them. The King used openly to say in the presence of his officers, doctors, and chiefs—"My sole object, oh wise Mullas, is to ascertain truth, to find out and disclose the principles of genuine religion, and to trace it to its divine origin.

Take care, therefore, that through the influence of your human passions, you are not induced to conceal the truth; and say nothing contrary to the almighty decrees. If you do, you are responsible before God for the consequences of your impiety."

Previous to the time that this address was made, several doctors and theologians of Hindustan, such as Maulana 'Abdu-lla Sultanpuri, commondly known as Makhdumu-l Mulk, and Shaikh 'Abdu-n Nabi, the *Sadr* and others, were constantly present at Court, and received great favours from the King. The two learned men first mentioned were considered the best authorities on all questions pertaining to religion and law, but they frequently held opposite opinions to one another, and expressed themselves in tones of anger and recrimination, so that at last their credit and reputation declined in the King's estimation, and he became indifferent to the religion which they professed. The common people learning day after day something about the nature of the subjects discussed in these assemblages, could so little comprehend the real purpose for which they were held, that they misrepresented the King's object in encouraging them, and entertained suspicions of his motives which were derogatory to his character, and but little deserved.

DEATH OF BIRBAL[5]

In this year (994 A.H.), the victorious armies were sent, under the command of Raja Birbal, to put down the insurgent Yusufzais. A person came to the Raja, and told him that the Afghans intended to make a night attack upon his force, that the mountain pass did not extend beyond three or four *kos*, and that if he could traverse

[5]*The account which Elphinstone gives of this disaster is in exact accordance with that here given. The authority he gives is "Muntakhabu-t Tawarikh—Elphinstone, book ii. chap. ix.*

that distance he would be in safety. Birbal, without communicating with Zain Khan, resolved to go through the pass, and setting his forces in motion, he arrived at the gorge about sunset. The Afghans assembled from all sides upon the summits of the pass with arrows and stones, and the royal forces, losing their way amid the darkness in the narrow defile, fell into the deep holes and abysses, and there perished. The royal army thus experienced a severe defeat, and nearly 8000 men were slain. Raja Birbal, who fled to save his life, was killed, and no trace of him was found. Zain Khan and Abu-l Fath were also defeated on the 5th Rabi'u-l awwal of the same year, and with great difficulty made their way to Atak. This defeat had great effect upon the mind of the Emperor, and several times he refused to see (these commanders). Raja Todar Mal was chosen to head a well-appointed force, and repair this disaster. The Raja advanced into the mountains with great skill, where he erected several forts, and he conducted the campaign with such consummate judgment, that the Afghans were soon driven back, and kept within narrow bounds.

CURIOUS WORK OF ART

One of the wonders of art which was exhibited during this year (A.H. 1003) was the work of Saiyid Hussain Shirazi. He used to stand with a box in his hand, and when any one gave him a rupee, he threw it into the box, and it kept on rolling until it fell to the bottom. Upon this, a parrot which was chained to it began to speak, and two fowls began also to cackle at one another. Then a small window opened, at which a panther put out its head, and let a shell fall from its mouth into a dish which was placed on a lion's head, and the shell then came out of the lion's mouth. A short time elapsed, when another windows opened, and another lion came forth, took the shell in its mouth and retired, and the windows again closed. Two elephants then appeared with perfect trunks, and there were also two figures of men, who sounded drums. A rope then thrust itself forward, and again retreated, of its own accord. Two other men then advanced and made obeisance. Shortly after, another window opened, and a puppet came forth with an ode of Hafiz in its hand, and when the ode was taken away from the puppet, it retired, and the window was closed. In short, whenever a piece of money was placed in the hands of Husain Shirazi, all these marvels were exhibited. The King first gave a gold *mohur* with his own hand, and withnessed the sight. He then ordered his attendants to give a rupee each. The odes which were presented were given by the King to Nakib Khan, by whom they were read out. This exhibition lasted for several nights.

FAMINE

During the year 1004 H. there was a scarcity of rain throughout the whole of Hindustan, and a fearful famine raged continuously for three or four years. The King ordered that alms should be distributed in all the cities, and Nawab Shaikh Farid Bokhari, being ordered to superintend and control their distribution, did all in his power to relieve the general distress of the people. Public tables were spread, and the army was increased, in order to afford maintenance to the poor people. A kind of plague also added to the horrors of this period, and depopulated whole houses and cities, to say nothing of hamlets and villages. In consequence of the dearth of grain and the necessities of ravenous hunger, men ate their own kind. The streets and roads were blocked up with dead bodies, and no assistance could be rendered for their removal.

THE EMPEROR WOUNDED

In this year also the King, while witnessing an antelope-fight, was wounded in the thigh by one of their horns, which penetrated very deep. Great alarm was felt throughout the country, but after retiring for a few days to the inner apartments, and seating himself on the carpet of affliction, he recovered, by the blessing of God, and restored comfort to the hearts of all the world.

CURIOUS APARTMENT

One of the curiosities exhibited this year was manufactured by the most celebrated physician of the time, Hakim 'Ali. It filled every beholder with wonderment, however wise he might be. He built a room about the ordinary breadth and length to which the only entrance was at the top, by a sort of trap-door. Over the roof of the room he constructed a reservoir, which remained full of water, and no one could enter the room except by plunging into the bath. Upon reaching this single entrance, he gained access to the room, which he found furnished with carpets, books, and all the conveniences of a sitting room,—yet no water by any chance ever got into it. It is said that the King one day with some of his private companions got into the room in the way above indicated, and after remaining there some time enjoying their conversation, left it again by the passage through that single-trap door.

RAUZATU-T TAHIRIN

OF

TAHIR MUHAMMAD

THE "Garden of the Immaculate," a general history by Tahir Muhammad bin Imadu-d din Hasan bin Sultan 'Ali bin Haji Muhammad Husain Sabzwari. It was commenced A.H. 1011 A.D. 1602-3, three years before the death of Akbar, and conclude A.H. 1015, A.D. 1606-7, after the accession of Jahangir; and as the year of the Hijra 1011 is numerically represented by *Rauzat,* the author, as he tells us in his preface, has combined that word with his own name, Tahir, to form the fanciful title he has given to his history.

The contents of the work are much the same as those of other general Asiatic histories. It begins with a copious Index which it is to be regretted other authors have not imitated. It extends to the 45th page, and serves as a chronological table, as it shows how long each sovereign reigned.

The *Rauzatu-t Tahirin* is divided into five Books (*kism*), sub-divided into Chapters (*bab*), and Sections (*fasl*). Some of these Sections are more minutely subdivided, not for the mere purpose of showing the author's ingenuity, but because the different dynasties treated of really required the distinction.

CONTENTS

Book I.—Comprises an account of the creation, forty prophets, twenty-two ancient sages, Persian and Arabic Dynasties before Muhammad, including the Peshdadians. Kaianians, Ashkanians, Sassanians, and Ghassanians. In three chapters: from p. 45 to p. 641.

Book II.—The Khalifas, and the Dynasties which rose

under the 'Abbasides, such as the Tahirides, Samanians. Buwaihides or Dailamites, Ghaznivides, Ghorians, Kara-khatayans, Saljukians, Atabaks, etc. In four chapters:—from p. 641 to p. 826.

Book III.—The Dynasties of Tatars, Mughals, and Turks, Osmanlis of Constantinople, Changiz Khan, Timur, and their predecessors and descendants, with several other Dynasties, including the Kara-kuinlu and Ak-kuinlu[6] rulers and the Safavi Kings of Persia. In seven chapters: from p. 826 to p. 981.

Book IV.—"On the Rulers of India, previous to the introduction of Muhammadanism, called the Brahmans of Hind; who, when troubles and disorganization prevailed, made their appearance, as person endowed with every excellence, for the regeneration of the country. Their appearance is called *Avatar*, of which there have been nine from the beginning of the creation until now, i.e., from the Fish *Avatar* down to Krishna *Avatar*."

Abstract of the *Mahabharata* and *Harbans Puran* (*Harivansa*); the history of the Surajbans and Chandarbans Rajas, and those who succeeded them. In two chapters and a conclusion.

Book V.—The Sultans of India, beginning with the Slave Kings, and ending with Akbar, and an account of his contemporaries, comprising fourteen nobles, fifty-seven poets, twenty-four doctors and philosophers; the rulers of Sind, Multan, Kashmir, Gujarat, Malwa, Dakhin, Jaunpur, and Bengal; the wonders of the islands and ports near Bengal, including an account of Ceylon, Pegu, Arrakan, Kuch Bihar and Portugal. In four Chapters: from p. 981 to p. 1200. The last chapter contains something about the author himself.

SIZE—Folio, 1200 pages, containing 23 lines in a page.

It will appear, therefore, that Book V., or about

[6]*It might have been added that Briggs gives it as Koovinloo* (*Firishta, iii.* 341), *which Hammer-Purgstall*

one-sixth of the entire work, is devoted to India; but as it contains in that portion little that is not equally well told elsewhere, it is not of much value, except as a useful compendium. It is unfortunate that the only useful portion of this Book, namely, the third chapter on Indian Biographies, is not included in the volume. A more serious hiatus occurs in the exclusion of the whole of Book IV., though there is no break in the paging. This, as well as the biographical portion, may form separate volumes, for they are not included in two copies which I have consulted, though I have found them in a Lucknow copy.

The work is most copious in the legendary history of Persia, which is contained in Book I., comprising more than half the entire volume.

The chief authorities quoted in the work, are the *Jami'u-t Tawarikh, Rauzatu-s Safa, Tarikh-i Guzida, 'Lubbu-t Tawarikh, Tarikh-i Nizami,* the *Zafar-nama,* Ghaffari's *Nigaristan,* and the *Bahman-nama;* and from these, several chapters are copied verbatim.

Of the few copies which I know of this history, one is in the possession of Shahzada Mirza Ghulam Fakhru-d din Bahadur, son of the King of Dehli; the second is in the Asiatic Society's Library, containing only the first three Books; the third is in the Library of Nawab Siraju-l Mulk, minister of Haidarabad, labelled with the name of Tarikh-i Tahiri, under which it is often quoted by those authors who have consulted the work. There is also one at Mirat and one in the Moti Mahall Library at Lucknow. There is an imperfect copy labelled *Shigarf-nama* at the latter place. Nawab 'Ali Muhammad Khan Jhajjari's copy contains 1193 pp. of 23 lines, and is probably the copy above noticed as belonging to

characterizes as being "in accordance with his usual perverse method of spelling."—(Jahrbucher, No. li. p. 56.)

the Shahzada. A personal examination shows that this imperfect copy is thus devided:

Book I. to p. 628. Book II. to p. 860. Book III. to p. 960. Book IV. Book V. p. 960 to p. 1193. It does not contain biographies.

Major Stewart mentions it in his Catalogue,[7] but though he divides it into five Books, it is evident from his table of contents that his volume comprises only the first three Books.

M. Fraehn classes the *Rauzatu-t Tahirin* among his desiderata.[8]

EXTRACTS

Sultan Mu'izzu-d din Muhammad Sam Ghori led his army into Gujarat, and in the first action overthrew Rai Bhoj Deo. In a second engagement between them, the Rai succeeded in defeating the Sultan; but in a third which ensued, Sultan Mu'izzu-d din completely routed his antagonist, and captured from him numerous elephants, together with all his regal equipage and property. On his return from Gujarat, he besieged Khusru Malik, the Ghaznivide, in Lahore, and took from him some elephants and treasure.

Next year he marched his troops in the same direction, and entirely subdued Lahore, and appointing his own deputies to govern it, returned to Ghazni.

In India he captured several forts, such as those of Sialkot and Sirhind, and garrisoned them with his own men. Next season Sultan Mu'izzu-d din made another expedition into India, and killed Raja Pithaura in a single action. He left Sultan Kutbu-d din Aibak, one of his favourite slaves, in the fort of Kuhram, and returned to Ghazni.

[7] *Descriptive Catalogue of Tippoo Sultan's Library, p.* 6.

[8] *Indications Bibliographiques, no.* 216.

The following year the Sultan came again to India, and proceeded to Kanauj, the Raja of which place he reduced, took possession of three hundred elephants, and appointed Sultan Kutbu-d din viceroy at Dehli. . . . .

Sultan Mu'izzu-d din soon after turned his attention towards reducing some disaffected Khokar chiefs, who had revolted on the confines of Lahore, during the Sultan's absence. Thence he advanced to Lahore, and recaptured the hills of Siwalik from the *zamindars*, and having ordered his army to Dehli under the command of Kutbu-d din Aibak, he left Lahore to return to Ghazni, but was assassinated at Damek on his way, in the month of Sha'ban, 602 A.H., by some Khokars who had vowed to accomplish this object. Sultan Mu'izzu-d din's reign lasted four years.

SULTAN MUHAMMAD 'ADIL[9]

On the death of Shah Muhammad (Farmuli) and his sons, Daulat Khan Lohani became so wealthy that, in imitation of Sultan Muhammad Tughlik Shah, he used to fill little vessels with pieces of gold and silver, and throw them in different parts of the city, and whoever was fortunate enough to secure one of these vessels received the sum of 500 *tankas* from the royal treasury on presenting it.[10]

The nobles and officers of the army, finding Sultan

[9]*The Extract which appeared in the old volume has been reduced to the following short passage, retained as a specimen. The whole of it is borrowed from the Tabakat-i Akbari.*

[10]*Other authors say that arrows tipped with precious metal were dispersed and paid for at the above value, and with much more probability they ascribe the extravagant folly to Muhammad 'Adil, whose ignorance and absurdity obtained for him the nickname of 'Adali (the foolish).*

Muhammad neglectful of the administration of the country, each assumed independence in his own country. Himun, by caste a Bania, inhabitant of Rewari, having ingratiated himself with the monarch, was appointed commander-in-chief of his army, and Shamshir Khan, a slave of Shir Khan, was invested with the title of Daulat Khan. Taj Khan Kirani, with 'Imad and Sulaiman his brothers, revolted against the Sultan, and fled from Gwalior towards Bihar and Bengal. Sultan Muhammad 'Adali being informed of their proceedings, detached some forces to pursue them closely. They came to action near Kanauj, where Taj Khan was defeated, and fled towards Chunar, and shut himself up in that exceedingly strong fortress. Himun, accompanied by a large army, and well supplied with elephants, crossed the river Ganges, defeated these nobles, and captured the fort of Chunar, and fully established the Sultan's power by these repeated successes.

About this time Ibrahim Khan, son of Ghazi Khan Sur, who was cousin of 'Adali, and had married his sister, took alarm and fled to Bayana. Sultan Muhammad despatched 'Isa Khan Niazi to chastise him. An action ensued in the vicinity of Kalpi, in which 'Isa Khan Niazi was defeated. Ibrahim Khan then repaired to Dehli, where he assumed the title of Sultan Ibrahim Shah, caused the *khutba* to be read and money to be coined in his own name, and extended his authority over several towns and districts.

In consequence of this rebellion, Sultan Muhammad 'Adali was compelled to suspend his expedition against the Kiranis, and marched, without intermission, to the banks of the Jumna, where he encamped.

MUNTAKHABU-T TAWARIKH

OR

AHSANU-L TAWARIKH

OF

HASAN BIN MUHAMMAD

THIS common title of *Muntakhabu-t Tawarikh* has been bestowed upon his General History by Hasan bin Muhammad al-Khaki al-Shirazi, who came to India in the time of Akbar, and obtained different offices under the government. He tells us that from his early youth he imbibed a great taste for historical literature, which was so much increased on his arrival in India, "the abode of security," that he determined to write a work, which should embrace in one volume an account of the Prophets, Saints, Sultans, Philosophers, Poets, and Wazirs. He has certainly fulfilled his intention as far as comprehensiveness goes, for he includes in it all the known Dynasties of Asia; but the separate biographies, except of the Prophets and Sultans, seem to have been overlooked. The compilation is of little use to the Indian historian.

His authorities are many and good; some of them not to be found without difficulty in these days. He mentions the *Rauzatu-s Safa, Habibu-s Siyar. Mujmal Fasihi,* Ibn Khallikan, *Jahan-kushai, Tarikh-i Rashidi* of Mirza Haidar Kashmiri. *Akbar-nama, Tarikh-i Nizami, Tarikh-i Firoz-shahi* of Zia Barni, *Tabakat-i Nasiri, Tarikh-i Binakiti, Jahan-ara,* and *Tarikh-i Abu-l Fazl Baihaki.* He states that he commenced the work before the close of Akbar's reign, and completed it in the fifth year of Jahangir's, A.H. 1019 (A.D. 1610-11), in which year, as he tells us at the close of his history, he was appointed *diwan* of Patna.

Elphinistone quotes a book bearing this title, which he says was writen in 1004 H., and is probably the same work as this. Briggs also quotes it in some of his notes to the subordinate dynasties. (The account which Elphinstone gives of the death of Birbal, and for which he refers to this work, is in exact accordance with that translated from Nuru-l Hakk elsewhere. They were probably derived from a common source.)[11]

The work consists of various detached histories not divided with the usual display of minute accuracy, into Books, Chapters, and Sections.

CONTENTS

The Prophets.—Ancient Persian Kings.—Kings of Babil and Assyria.—Israelites.—Yunan.—Himyarites.—Yumen.—Ghassan.—Hirah.—Turkish Kings from Japhet.—Tatars.—Mughals.—Muhammad and the first Khalifas.—Imans.—Ummayides.— 'Abbasides. — Tahirites. —Aghlabites.—Tulunites.—Ikhshidites.[12] — Hamadanites. —Saffarians.— Samanians.— Ghaznvides.— Atabaks.— Obaydites.—Khwarazm-shahis.—Ghorians and Kings of Dehli.—Aiyubites.—Kings of the Arabs.—Rulers of Turkistan before Changiz Khan.—Changiz Khan and his descendants.—Various Rulers of Persia, Ilkhanians, etc., etc.—Various Rulers of India, viz., Dakhin, Gujarat, Malwa, Khandesh, Bengal, Jaunpur, Kashmir, Sind, Multan. Osmanlis of Constantinople, Gurganians, Babar, Humayun, Akbar, Jahangir, and Safi Kings of Persia.

SIZE.—Small folio, containing 884 pages of 17 lines each; but the codex is here and there defective, and the history of the *Safi, Sufi,* or *Safavi* kings of Persia, men-

[11]*Elphinstone, vol. ii., pp.* 151, 292. *The work is also quoted in the Jinanu-l Firdans.*

[12]*For an account of these Dynasties, see M. de Guignes, Hist. des Huns, tom. iii. pp.* 124-154.

tioned in the copious table of contents, occupying nearly six pages of the preface, is not bound up with this volume. A note in the beginning of the volume states that it contains 522 folios, which was probably the correct number before the abstractions.

Of the portions relating to India, the history of the Ghaznivides occupies from fol. 86v. to fol. 90v.;—the ancient history of the Ghorains, and the Kings of Dehli, from Shahabu-d din to Ibrahim bin Sikandar Lodi, from fol. 141r. to fol. 157v.;—the minor Dynasties of India, from fol. 262v. to fol. 344r.; of which Gujarat occupies 18 folios, and Kashmir 20 folios. The account of Babar begins at fol. 372r., Humayun 373r., Akbar 385v., and Jahangir 437v.

In these latter portions he has been very particular with regard to his dates, his official duties having probably taught him the value of correctness in such matters; for in the two short Extracts which follow, we find him at one time a pay-master, and at another a revenue accountant.

This work is rare. There is a copy of some antiquity in the Moti Mahall Library at Lucknow. The Tonk Nawab has one, and so has Muhammad Hasan of Cawnpore, and Fakir Nuru-d din of Lahore. Other copies have been heard of. Muhammad Hasan's copy contains the whole of the Safavi dynasty.

EXTRACTS

On the 5th Shahryur, 1003 A.H., Muzaffar Husain Mirza, son of Sultan Husain Mirza, son of Bahram Mirza Safavi, arrived from his *jagir* of Khandahar at the Court of the Emperor Akbar, and was appointed an *amir* of 5000. He had four sons, Bahram, Sadar, Alfas, and Tahmasp Mirza. The *sarkar* of Sambhal was assigned to him in *jagir*, and Kandahar to Shah Beg Khan Kabuli.

On Saturday, the 9th Safar, 1004 A.H., Shaikh Faizi, "the chief of poets," died. He was born on the 1st

Sha'ban, 954 A.H. The year 1004 A.H. was marked also by the death of Hakim (Humam), brother of Hakim Abu-l Fath, and by Prince Shah Murad's conquest of Berar, a province of the Dakhin within the government of Nizamu-l Mulk. On the 18th Murdad of this year, a deer gored the Emperor, and hurt one of his testicles. The pain was very excruciating for twenty-nine days, and his danger created a sensation throughout Hindustan, until he was cured. Raja 'Ali Khan, ruler of Khandesh, was slain in battle this year in the Dakhin, where he was present with the royal army.

In the year 1005 A.H. a tent which was pitched in the palace on the occasion of the festival of *Nauroz*, caught fire, and the articles collected therein, according to custom on this festival, were consumed by the flames. On the 21st Farwardin, the Emperor proceeded on an excursion to Kashmir, where he sojourned for three months and twenty days. His Majesty afterwards came back to Lahore, and sent Prince Daniyal to Allahabad, to assume charge of the government of that *suba*. He was honoured with a *mansab* of 7000, and Kalij Khan was appointed his private tutor. In this year Mirza Rustam, son of Prince Shah Murad, died at Lahore, after a severe illness of six years and three months.

On the 17th of Shahryur, 1006 A.H., the Emperor appointed Rai Hardas to act as minister conjointly with Khwaja Shamsu-d din.

On the 23rd Aban of this year, Minuchihr Beg, with five hundred Kazilbash horse, waited upon the Emperor at Lahore, as ambassador from Shah 'Abbas, accompanied Mir Ziau-l Mulk, who had been sent to Shah 'Abbas by the Emperor on a mission, in company with Yadgar Sultan.

On the 26th of this month the Emperor left Lahore for Agra, with the view of expediting the conquest of the Dakhin.

On the 22nd of Urdibihisht Prince Shah Murad died

in the Dakhin. On the 2nd of the month Tir, Prince Daniyal was sent to subdue the Dakhin. In the latter part of this year Asaf Khan was honoured with the post of general *diwan*.

On the 6th of Mihr, 1007 A.H., the Emperor having placed Agra under the protection of Kalij Khan, marched towards the Dakhin. Sultan Salim was sent to Ajmir, accompanied by Raja Man Singh and Shah Kuli Khan Mahram, to chastise the *amirs* under the Rana of Udipur. In this year the Emperor granted Gujarat in *jagir* to the Khan-i 'Azam, and deputed Mirza Shamshi, the eldest son of the Khan-i 'Azam, to settle the affairs of that province. The writer of this history was sent from the neighbourhood of Dahapur, to take charge of the office of paymaster at Gujarat.

In 1008 A.H. Khwaja Shamsu-d din, who, after the march of the Emperor to Agra, had been appointed to the office of the *diwan* of the Panjab, expired. In the same year Prince Salim, who had been directed to chastise the Rana of Udipur, assumed the title of King when he reached the neighbourhood of Allahabad, plundered the treasury of Bihar, which contained three *lacs* of rupees, and resumed all the *jagirs* which had been bestowed upon the servants of the Court.

On the 6th of the month Shahryur of this year Ahmadnagar in the Dakhin was taken by Prince Daniyal. Mirza Shah-rukh, the Khan-i Khanan. Mirza Yusaf Khan. and others.

[13]On Sunday, the 14th of Safar, 1019 A.H., an individual of the name of Kutb, born in Ujah[14] of Multan and who, by styling himself Sultan Khusru, had gained over a considerable number of lawless Ujjaini Rajputs

[13]*This account occurs in the fifth year of the Memoirs, p. 182, where it is said the imposition was made more perfect by showing the marks on his eyes where they had been burnt.* [14]*Uch.*

to make common cause with him, entered the city of Patna, and made himself master of it, as well as of its fort, in consequence of the absence in Gorakhpur of the Governor of Bihar, named Afzal Khan, son of Shaikh Abu-l Fazl. The treasure which was in the fort was distributed among his troops. Afzal Khan, on learning these circumstances, made forced marches, and on Friday, the 19th Safar, reached the banks of the Punpun, eight miles from Patna, Kutb, with the design of forcing him to an engagement, came out of the city, and a bloody battle ensued, in which Kutb was defeated. He then fled and sought safety within the fort, which at length fell into the hands of the governor, when Kutb was taken prisoner and put to death, on Sunday, the 21st of Safar.

After a month, orders were issued by the Emperor, directing that Ilyas Bahadur, 'Inayat Beg Diwan, Shaikh Hasam of Benares, and several others who had dastardly fled from Patna, although the protection of that city had been committed to their charge by Afzal Khan, should be paraded on asses all the way to Agra, with their heads and beards entirely shorn off, and dressed in female apparel.[15]

The writer of this history was at this time sent to Patna, the *diwani* of that place having been conferred on him.

[15] *A similar punishment occurs in the Jahan-kusha, when Jalalu-d din punished those who deserted him in the action at Baghdad.—Price, vol. ii. p.* 415; *Briggs, vol. iii. p.* 459; *Matla'u-s Sa'dain, p.* 173.

MA-ASIR-I RAHIMI

OF

MUHAMMAD 'ABDU-L BAKI

Dr. Lee observes of this work, that "it is a valuable and elaborate history of the Emperors and other eminent men of Tartary, Hindustan, etc., by Muhammad 'Abdu-l Bakiu-l Rahimiu-l Nahavandi. In large folio, containing about 4000 pages."[1] Major Stewart describes it as "Memoirs of 'Abdu-l Rahim Khan, Khan-khanan, *wazir*, and of all the illustrious nobles, authors, and poets, who resided at the Court of Akbar. Author, 'Abdu-l Baki, A.D. 1613."[2]

These authors differ much in their account of the work: both are partly right and partly wrong. There is no account of the Emperors and other eminent men of Tartary, if we except the account of 'Abdu-r Rahim's ancestors, and the biographical details do not concern the Court of Akbar, but belong almost entirely to the Dakhin. A great portion of the work is devoted to an ample detail of the transactions of his patron, the Khan-khanan, his sons and progenitors, who though he certainly was of sufficient eminence to deserve a full biography, it is here written, as usual under such circumstances, in so fulsome a strain of eulogy, that it is difficult to know what faith to put in it. The first Book contains Indian History, not sufficiently comprehensive to be of any essential service; but it is so far valuable that it does not literally copy Firishta, which can rarely be said of any other author who has followed in the same line.

[1]*Travels of Ibn Batuta*, p. xiv.

[2]*Descriptive Catalogue of Tippo Sultan's Library*, p. 14.

Nizamu-d din is his great guide, and his alarm at attempting any period of history not already occupied by another is shown by the Extract taken from the close of his account of Akbar. The work also contains a *Tazkira,* or notices of poets, with long extracts from their writings, and it will be seen from the following Table of Contents that nearly one-third of the volume is devoted to that object;—the accounts of the poets extending from p. 990 to p. 1454.

CONTENTS: Preface, pp. 1-7. Introduction, respecting the ancestors of 'Abdu-r Rahim, Khan-khanan, pp. 7-36. Book I.—An account of Muhammad Bairam Beg, father of 'Abdu-r Rahim, preceded by the history of the Kings of Hindustan from the time of the Ghaznivides to the accession of Jahangir, including the Kings of Bengal, p. 46,—the Kings of Jaunpur, p. 52,—Kings of Malwa, p. 56,—Kings of Kashmir, p. 113,—Kings of Multan, p. 148,—Kings of Dehli, p. 160,—Babar, p. 272,—Humayun, p. 290,—Akbar, p. 381,—Jahangir, p. 552;—pp. 37-606. Book II.—The virtues and victories of 'Abdu-r Rahim, with copies of *farmans* addressed to him, and of some of his compositions, including also an account of the rulers of Gujarat, p. 621,—of Sind, p. 496,—of Dakhin, p. 776,—of Khandesh, p. 808;—pp. 602-922. Book III.—On the palaces, baths, mosques, and other buildings erected by the Khan-khanan, the gardens planted by him, and the ships built by him;—pp. 923-932. Book IV.—An account of the sons of the Khan-khanan, pp. 933-968. Conclusion in a Preface and three[3] Chapters, (1) on contemporary philosophers, physicians, and other celebrated men, 31 persons, p. 962: (2) poets, including the author, 92 persons, p. 990; (3) on the mili-

[3] *In the body of the work the Chapters are said to amount to four; but the Preface states that the Conclusion is divided into three Chapters, and the detail shows that there are only three.*

tary officers under command of the Khan-khanan, 44 persons, p. 1454; p. 969-1513. Size.—Folio, 1513 pages, each containing 25 lines. There are a few blank pages, which are about equal to the marginal additions.

The author, 'Abdu-l Baki, Nahavandi, composed his work under the encouragement he received from Abu-l Faiz Faizi, brother of Abu-l Fazl, and 'Abdu-r Rahim, Khan-khanan son of Bairam Khan. He gives a little information respecting himself and his ancestry, referring for more copious particulars to Takiu-d din's *Tazkira,* entitled *Ma-asiru-l Khizria,* which was dedicated and named after his brother, Agha Khizr, and to 'Abdu-l Ma'ali's *Tazkira,* which is dedicated to Shah 'Abbas; and as "self-praise is a great fault," he refers to them, rather than repeat in this work what they have said respecting him. In them also will be found a full account of his family and connexions, as well of his patron, the Khan-khanan. His family was originally from Julak,[4] "which contains more than 30,000 houses," but in consequence of the contentions which arose during the reign of Shah Ismail Safavi, his family left Julak, and went to reside at Nahavand.

The author states that his ancestors were Generals under Afrasiyab, and that they held the lands of Julak in rent-free tenure from Shah Ismail. His most noted ancestor was Aka Baba, who resided at Hamadan. His brother was made Deputy Governor of Hamadan in the time of Shah 'Abbas. Amir Taki Muhammad has noticed the excellence of his administration in the *Tazkira* which he has written, and many memorials of his munificence exist in the neighbourhood, especially the embankment at Kashan and the avenue of trees, of which our author for a long time enjoyed the proceeds.

He appears, for some reason or other, to have given

[4]*For the correct mode of writing this word, see Ousley's Persian Travels,* vol. ii, p. 3.

dissatisfaction to the reigning monarch, Shah 'Abbas; on account of which he determined upon quitting his native country, and, at the invitation of Abu-l Faiz Faizi and 'Abdu-r Rahim Khan, was induced to visit Hindustan, and arrived at Burhanpur in Khandesh in A.H. 1023, where he was received with kindness, and presented with a *jagir*. He completed his work in A.H. 1025 (A.D. 1616), calling it *Ma-asir-i Rahimi,* after his patron, in whose praise he has inserted many pieces of poetry in the body of the work, and declares his intention of continuing these laudatory effusions till the day of his death.

This work is not common in India. There is one copy at Lahore, in two volumes, which is an abridgment, rather than the entire work. The copy which the Asiatic Society possesses constitutes one of the most valuable manuscripts of its collection. It was transcribed in a legible *nasta'lik* hand under the author's own superintendence, and contains revisions and marginal additions in his own handwriting. It purports to have been sent as a present to his friend, Khwaja Sultan Muhammad Isfahani, in the year 1026 H., and afterwards to have been received from him again, and presented in 1041 H. to Kazi 'Abdu-l 'Aziz. The author states that this MS. has not undergone the careful revision he could wish, and that a complete history of the Kings of the Dakhin is wanting, which he hopes to supply some future day.

EXTRACT[5]

The King went out for the purpose of hunting and arrived at Sultanpur, on the bank of the river, thirty *kos*

[5]*The Extracts which appeared in the old volume relating to Kai-Kubad and to Mubarak Kutbu-d din were abstracts of Zia-Barni. That relating to "the building of a private chapel," and that containing the record of the events of the 38th Ilahi year after the accession," were copied from the Tabakat-i Akbari.*

from Lahore, and the Khan-khanan, who had gone to Sirhind to pay his respects to Prince Daniyal, was sent for by the King to be consulted. He had an interview with His Majesty near Shaikhpur, and had frequent conferences on the subject of the Dakhin, when the King inquired whether that province could not be conquered without troubling the Prince to go there. The Khan-khanan undertook to subdue it, and instructions were therefore issued, that the army, which had been directed to accompany the Prince, should be placed under the orders of the Khan-khanan. The Prince was then summoned to Court, which he reached in two days. The Khan-khanan, loaded with honours by the King, set out on his expedition, and His Majesty, having broken up his hunting camp, returned to Lahore. The Khan-khanan set out with all haste, and arrived at Agra. The rainy season was approaching, and he had received orders to draw what he could from the Agra treasury, to pay the soldiers, and provide for the conquest of the Dakhin. He remained at Agra during the rains, and having supplied himself with every necessary, he set out for Malwa, which was the *jagir* of Mirza Shah Rukh, with whom he had an interview in Ujjain. From Malwa he went to Khandesh, and by peaceful means induced Raja 'Ali Khan to declare his allegiance to the King. Khandesh thus became included in the subject states, and the coin was struck and the *khutba* read in the name of His Majesty in the country where Asir had baffled every attempt to subdue it. Khandesh was given in *jagir* to Raja 'Ali Khan, and he was enrolled among the nobles of 5,000. The Khan-khanan sent a petition from Raja 'Ali Khan, accompanied by a suitable offering, to His Majesty, that this grant might be confirmed, and that Raja 'Ali Khan might be recokoned among the royal adherents, and be allowed to accompany the army to the Dakhin. The King acceded to these proposals, and the Khan-khanan was rewarded with fresh marks of favour.

After the annexation of Khandesh, the Khan-khanan set out on his expedition to the Dakhin. His first step was to lay siege to Ahmadnagar. Chand Bibi, who was at that time ruler of that province, made peace under which the territory of Birar was surrendered to Akbar.

On the second occasion, when he attacked Ahmadnagar, Suhail, the Abyssinian. was appointed by 'Adil Shah, to the command of the army, and the armies of Nizamu-l Mulk, 'Adil Khan, Kutbu-l Mulk, and the Barid-Shahi chief being placed under his command, he came out in considerable strength and confidence. The Khan-khanan, with the little force at his command, fought like Rustam and Isfandiyar, and obtained a complete victory over Suhail. He then proceeded to the seige of Ahmadnagar, which he reduced, and brought the whole province of the Dakhin under the rule of the Emperor. As the conquests of the Dakhin, Khandesh, and Birar have already been fully detailed among the great achievements of the Khan-khanan in this book, I beg to refer thereto. If I were here to commence an account of this commander's proceedings in the Dakhin, it would extend to too great a length.

To be brief, the King reigned for fifty-two years over the whole of Hindustan, from Bengal to the extreme borders of Sind and Kandahar, and Zamindawar, and even to the shores of the sea. All the stubborn chiefs, *rajas, rais* and *zamindars* in Hindustan, including the Kings of Gujarat, Sind, Dakhin, Kashmir, Bengal, Malwa, and other countries, were made subject to his rule. Some, after defeat in action, some, under treaties of peace, were all in the end deprived of the exercise of independent sovereignty.

The author has extracted this account of the first thirty-eight years of the reign, viz., from A.H. 963 to 1002, from the *Tabakat-i Akbari,* by Nizamu-d din Ahmad Bakhshi, who was not spared to complete it. Of the remaining fourteen years the author has never seen any account; nor has he been able to procure information of the various events of that period. He has therefore omitted it from his history, and must refer to other authorities who may have written concerning this period.

Akbar was a powerful, world-subduing monarch, the very emblem of justice, to whose Court people from al sides resorted for protection, and to partake of a benevolence so universally diffused. He extended toleration to all religions and creeds, and would recognize no difference between them, his object being to unite all men in a common bond of peace. The names of the Sultans, nobles, ministers, poets, and philosophers who adorned his reign, can be ascertained from the *Tabakat-i Akbari* and the *Akbar-nama*; and in the same comprehensive works will be found an account of his greatness, and the inventions of his bright intellect and ready genius.

During his entire reign of fifty-two years, no neighbouring Prince of Hindustan made an incursion into his territories, and notwithstanding that the Afghan kings are notorious for their malignity and turbulence, they were not able to move from their homes during his supremacy, so that all quarters were subject to his victorious sword. Whoever dared to lift his head from loyalty and subjection never escaped with life.

Akbar died at Agra on the 23rd Jamadu-l awwal, A.H. 1014, after a reign of fifty-two years. The date of his death is found to be represented by the letters in the words "*faut-i Akbar Shah*," "the death of Akbar Shah."

ANFA'U-L AKHBAR
OF
MUHAMMAD AMIN

THIS work is of much the same historic character as the last. It is in a more abridged form, but is devoted to the eulogies of a patron, and their publication appears to have been one of the chief objects contemplated in the undertaking.

The author, Muhammad Amin, son of Daulat Muhammad-al Husaini-al Baliki, was in the service of Nawab Sipahdar Khan, who receives an enlarged and laudatory notice at the close of the work. He concluded it in A.H. 1036, and styled it *Anfa'u-l Akhbar,* "The most useful chronicle," because the year is represented by the letters composing those words. He resided chiefly at Ahmadnagar, on which account he often notices this city; and its buildings, gardens, and history, receive a large share of notice.

This history is divided into a Preface, ten Books, and a Conclusion. Contents: Preface.—Containing the usual lauds, pp. 1-6. Book I.—The early prophets, pp. 7-100. II.—The early philosophers, pp. 100-104. III.—The early Kings of Persia, pp. 104-135. IV.—The prophet Muhammad, pp. 136-138. V.—The four first Khalifs and twelve Imams, pp. 138-144. VI.—The Ummayide Khalifs, pp. 144-146. VII.—The 'Abbaside Khalifs, pp. 146-150. VIII.—The dynasties contemporary with, and subsequent to, the 'Abbaside Khalifs, viz. Tahirides,—Samanians, Buwaihides or Dailamites,—Isma'ilians,—Saljukians,—Ghorians,—and others, pp. 150-190. IX.—The sons of Japhet, pp. 191-218. X.—The dynasty of Timur.

The following are the rubrics of the tenth book.

Accession of Khakan Sa'id Shah Rukh, Sultan, to the throne of Khurasan.—Mirza 'Alau-d daula ascends the throne, and the death of Mirza 'Abdu-l Latif in the year 857 H.—Mirza Mughisu-d din Ulugh Beg Gurgan crosses the river.—March of Mirza Abu-l Kasim Babar to Khurasan.—Disagreement between Mirza 'Alau-d daula and Mirza 'Abdu-l Latif.—Enmity between Mirza Ulugh Beg and Mirza 'Abdu-l Latif; and the death of the King. —A brief account of Mirza Sultan Muhammad.—March of Mirza Balla.—Mirza 'Abdu-l Latif killed, and the accession of Mirza 'Abdu-lla to the throne of Samarkand.—Mirza 'Abdu-lla Shirazi killed.—and Sultan Sa'id ascends the throne.—March of Mirza Babar towards Balkh.—Mirza 'Alau-d Daula seized.—Mirza Sultan Muhammad. —Mirza Babar proceeds towards Astarabad.—Mirza Babar departs for Mashhad.—Mirza Shah Mahmud, and certain events of his time.—Arrival of Sultan Sa'id at Khurasan.—March of Mirza Ibrahim to Mazandarn, and his defeat by Mirza Jahan Shah Turkoman.—Visit of Mirza Jahan Shah to the capital of Khakan Sa'id, and his peace with him.—Fight of Sultan Sa'id with Mirzas Ibrahim, 'Alau-d Daula and Sanjar.—Arrival of Amir Khalil to besiege Hirat.—March of Sultan Sa'id towards Turkistan.—A brief account of Mirza Jahan Shah Turkoman.—March of Sultan Sa'id from Astarabad.—The Khurasani troops defeated and Sultan Sa'id Gurgan killed.—Accession of Sultan Husain Bahadur Khan to the throne.—Several events related in a concise manner.—March of Mirza Yadgar Muhammad with the design of conquest, and his defeat by the royal army.—The King marches against Mirza Yadgar Muhammad.—Accession of Mirza Yadgar Muhammad to the throne of Khurasan.—The King proceeds in the direction of the garden Zaghan, and Mirza Yadgar is killed.—Re-accession of the King to the throne of Khurasan.—The events which occurred after his accession to the throne of Khurasan.—Death of Mirza Sultan Husain, and the joint succession of Badiu-z

Zaman Mirza and Mirza Muzaffar Husain to the throne of Khurasan, and several other events.—A summary account of the tribe of Ak-Kuinlu who ruled in Azarbaijan, Fars, the two 'Iraks, and Kirman.—A brief account of the Uzbek Kings who ruled in Marwarau-n Nahr and Khurasan subsequent to 900 A.H.—Safavi Kings.—Conquests of 'Irak, Persia, and Kirman.—Fall of Baghdad, and flight of Sultan Murad.—Conquest of Khuzistan.—The territories of Khurasan conquered, and Shahi Beg Khan killed.—A brief acount of Amir Yar Muhammad Isfahani.—Arrival of Sultan Salim, King of Rum, in Iran.—Death of the King.—Accession of Shah Tahmasp, son of Shah Ismail· Zahiru-d din Muhammad Babar.—Accession of Humayun.—Capture of the fort of Champanir.—Sultan Bahadur.—The events which befell the King after his arrival at Agra.—Retreat of the King towards Iran, and several events which occurred at that time.—Return of the King from Iran towards Hindustan.—March of the King from Kabul in the direction of India, with the design of conquest.—Death of the King in Rabi'u-l awwal, 963 A.H.—Account of certain excellent men.—Biography of Muhammad Akbar, from the beginning of the first up to the fifty-first year of his reign.—An account of Jahangir.—Account of the King and certain events which occurred at that time.—Sultan Khusru fights, is defeated, and seized.—Return of Sultan Parwez from the Dakhin, and arrival of Sultan Khurram according to the summons of the King.—Rupture of engagements, and recurrence of the insurrection of Malik Ambar in the Dakhin.—Disaffection of Sultan Khurram.—An account of Sultan Khurram after his arrival in Bengal.—Settlement of the affairs of the Dakhin and march of the army to Bengal.—Misfortunes which occurred after the departure of Prince Sultan Parwez.—Fight of Sultan Parwez and Mahabat Khan with Sultan Khurram.—Submission of Malik Ambar.—Certain transactions related in a succinct manner.—Pp. 218-446. Conclusion.—Account of Sipahdar Khan.—The peace of God rest on him, and may his life be prolonged! Pp. 446-482. Size.—Small quarto, containing 482 pages, and 17 lines in each page. This work is probably unique. I know of only one copy, and that is an autograph of the author, transcribed in Muharram, 1037, only a few months after the composition of the original. This MS. belongs to Nawab Shamshir Kadr of Lucknow.

EXTRACTS

Reign of Akbar

In the year 1003 H. Prince Sultan Murad marched towards the Dakhin by order of the King, where Khwaja Beg Mirza and Mirza Muhammad Salih paid their respects to him. Upon the death of Prince Sultan Murad in the Dakhin, Prince Daniyal, as has already been mentioned in its proper place, went to that province and captured the fort of Ahmadnagar, which was the capital of Nizamu-l Mulk. The government of that country was conferred upon Khwaja Beg Mirza and Mirza Muhammad Salih. These two great men had resided in this country for a long period, during which they have conferred many kindnesses, obligations, and comforts upon the people, as will shortly appear in the sequel.

The forty-ninth, fiftieth, and fifty-first years of the reign of Akbar, or the years 1012, 1013, and 1014 of the Hijra were marked by the following events, viz:

In the year 1012, A.H. Prince Sultan Salim was imprisoned in bath, on the very day on which His Royal Highness, repenting of his evil actions, presented himself to the King, availing himself of the opportunity which the death of his grandmother, Mariam Makani, afforded him of offering his condolences to His Majesty. He was, however, after a space of twelve days, released. This year is also marked by the arrival from the Dakhin of the news of the death of Sultan Daniyal. In the year 1013 A.H., the King (Akbar) was taken ill. On Wednesday, the 12th of Jumada-s sani, 1014 A.H. he died at Agra, and was interred in Sikandra. "It is God alone who will exist for ever."

This King never sustained a defeat at any place. His army was victorious in every engagement. He subjugated all adversaries, some by means of arms, and some by peaceful means. The whole length and breadth of the land was firmly and righteously governed. All people of every description and station came to his Court, and universal peace being established among all classes, men of every sect dwelt secure under his protection. Be it not concealed that this account of his happy reign does not comprise even one-tenth part of the transactions which actually occurred in it. The detailed particulars of his reign are recorded in the *Akbar-nama* and the *Tarikh-i Nizami*. God be praised that the distress which the people experienced at the loss of their sovereign Akbar, was removed by the accession of his excellent and powerful son Jahangir. May this exalted dynasty maintain its power till the day of judgment!

REIGN OF JAHANGIR

A brief account follows of the events which occurred in the year 1036 H., viz.: When Mahabat Khan returned from the Dakhin by command of the King, His Majesty was in Kashmir. On the way a dispute arose between Mahabat Khan and Asaf Khan, son of I'timadu-d Daula, and brother of Nur Jahan Begam. It took so serious a turn, that they at last came to action, drawing up their troops in battle array. Mahabat Khan gained the victory, and Asaf Khan fled to the fort of Attak Benares, where he fortified himself. The victorious party besieged him, and after a few days succeeded in obtaining possesion of his person, when they took him to their master, who threw him into prison. These circumstances gained Mahabat Khan such influence at Court, that no one without his authority could go near the King, and His

Majesty's food and drink were subject to his inspection. Mahabat Khan also appointed his own obedient Rajputs to remain in constant attendance day and night on the King, thereby cutting off every one from direct communication with His Majesty. The matter stood upon this footing for about six months, when a party of Mughals, collected through the judicious counsels of the wise Nur Jahan Begam, marched against Mahabat Khan, put nearly 3000 of his Rajputs to death, and effected the release of Asaf Khan. Mahabat Khan being thus defeated took to flight. The Khan-khanan was sent by the King with a large force to pursue and exterminate him; but while engaged in the expedition, the Khan-khanan died and Mahabat Khan is in consequence still (i.e. the close of the year 1036 H.) wandering about with a small body of adherents.

Sultan Khurram remains in the Dakhin under the same circumstances as have been already mentioned. We must wait to see what may happen to him, and what course he may hereafter pursue.

This year is also marked by the death of Prince Parwez in the city of Burhanpur. The date of the death of that excellent Prince is found in the following chronogram, composed by Maulana Samadi Buanati, viz. *Shah-i Shahan bi-shud az jahan*. "The king of kings has departed from this world."

In this year Nizamu-l Mulk created a disturbance in the Dakhin, which, however, was put down by the exertions of Khan Jahan. A detail of this transaction will be found elsewhere.

At the present time, i.e., the latter part of the year, 1036 H., the people of this country, whether rich or poor, high or low, are in the enjoyment of all the blessings of comfort and content, and slumbering secure from all danger, are in return offering up their prayers to the Almighty God for the continued prosperity of the King, who is the safeguard of the empire, and the shadow of God.

THE CONCLUSION

The concluding part of this book contains an account of Sipahdar Khan; may the peace of God be on him! The object of giving an account of him in this work is that his memory may descend to posterity. Be it not concealed that his birthplace is Tabriz, and his ancestors were reckoned among the nobles of that country. His name is Mirza Muhammad Salih. In the year 1000 H. he left Iran for Hindustan, in company with the late Khwaja Beg Mirza, son of Masum Beg Safavi, who requires no eulogy, and whose excellent qualities cannot be adequately described. The relations of friendship and amity which subsisted between them were exceedingly strong.

Mirza Muhammad Salih, after his arrival in India, obtained the honour of an interview with His Majesty. *Mansabs* suitable to his dignity, as well as the government of the *suba* of Gujarat were conferred on him. While in Gujarat, he saw in a dream a white flag so lofty that it penetrated the very heavens; at one time it went towards his right hand, at another towards the left; then it retreated a short distance from him, and again approaching him, began to bend down towards him, when he seized hold of it with his hand, and placed it in an erect posture; upon which he woke from his dream. Since the time he had this auspicious dream, he has prospered day by day, and has attained his present exalted position. But the height of the flag presages to him, according to the interpretation of the dream, even a higher dignity than that which he has yet attained. He is constantly in the habit of relating this dream to intelligent persons. "There is a dignity yet greater than thine, and thy dignity at every period is not always the same. Wait till the dawn of fortune cometh to thee, as these are the mere harbingers of that dawn. The dignity which thou hast attained is very low, when compared with that which Fate yet ordains for thee in its full accomplishment."

THE END